edexcel
advancing learning, changing lives

Edexcel

DiDA

Diploma in Digital Applications

Access to
Using ICT

Elaine Topping

Ann Weidmann

Marilyn Hartwell

Contents

Preparing for DiDA

Look around you. You are surrounded by information: in the post, on the bus, in the classroom, everywhere!

Most of this information is produced using ICT.

In Unit 1, you will learn how to use ICT to work with information and get your message across to different audiences.

You will learn how to produce publications for screen and paper including leaflets, posters, reports, presentations and webpages.

Unit 1 will help you think clearly about:

▶ what you want to say

▶ who you want to say it to

▶ how you want to say it.

In this chapter you will learn:

▶ *what qualifications you can get as a DiDA student*

▶ *how DiDA units are assessed*

▶ *how to use this book and CD*

▶ *what you need to learn for Unit 1*

▶ *how to keep you and your work safe.*

What is DiDA?

DiDA offers a number of different units, each worth one GCSE. The qualification you get depends on how many units you complete. At the moment you can get an Award, a Certificate or a Diploma.

Achieving the Award

Unit 1: Using ICT is the basic toolkit for DiDA. If you work through this set of materials and you can apply your ICT skills effectively, you could get an **Award in Digital Applications (AiDA)**.

Achieving the Certificate

The **Certificate in Digital Applications (CiDA)** can be achieved by adding any other unit to Unit 1. The optional units are shown in the table.

Unit	Title	In this unit students learn how to:
2	Multimedia	gather digital assets (sound, images, video, animation etc) and combine them to create multimedia products
3	Graphics	produce effective images for screen and print
4	ICT in Enterprise	use ICT to plan and promote an enterprise activity

Further units will be offered in the future.

Achieving the Diploma

The **Diploma in Digital Applications (DiDA)** is achieved by completing Unit 1 plus any three other units.

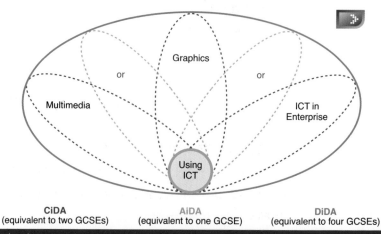

CiDA
(equivalent to two GCSEs)

AiDA
(equivalent to one GCSE)

DiDA
(equivalent to four GCSEs)

What's in DiDA? This diagram shows how the qualification works. Watch the animation to see how everything fits together.

How difficult is it?

You can take each unit at Level 1 or Level 2. This is one of the things that makes DiDA special. For example, if you are very good at multimedia, but not so good at graphics, you can do Unit 2 (Multimedia) at Level 2 and Unit 3 (Graphics) at Level 1. You will get an Award, Certificate or Diploma at Level 1 or Level 2. What DiDA qualification you end up with depends on what marks you get in each unit.

How is DiDA assessed?

DiDA students do not have to sit a formal exam. Once you have completed the work needed for a unit, you will have around 30 hours at your centre to work on a project set by the exam board. This project is called an SPB. SPB stands for Summative Project Brief and this will give you your task for the assessed project. Each SPB is published as a website so it can be read on screen.

So what will you have to do?

The SPB for Unit 1 will have a scenario and a series of activities based on it. You will use ICT to develop a range of publications for different audiences and purposes, both on screen and in print. Have a look at a Level 1 SPB published by Edexcel to get an idea of what is involved.

The final stage of the SPB is to create an electronic portfolio (eportfolio) to demonstrate your achievements. This will allow others to view your publications on screen and see evidence of how you produced them. Your eportfolio will be marked by your teacher and checked by a moderator.

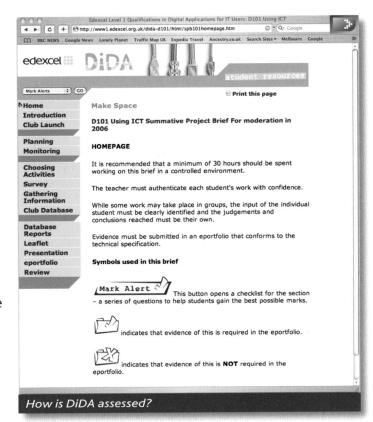

What grades can you get?

All DiDA units can be awarded at four levels – Pass, Credit, Merit and Distinction. They are all equivalent to GCSE grades, as this table shows:

GCSE grade	DiDA Level 1	DiDA Level 2
A*		Distinction
A		Merit
B		Credit
C	Distinction	Pass
D	Merit	
E	Credit	
F/G	Pass	

There is an overlap between Level 1 and Level 2. A distinction at Level 1 requires the same level of work as a pass at Level 2.

How do you use the ActiveBook?

There is a printed book for you to read, and there is also a CD which contains the pages from the printed book and lots of extra material. This electronic version of the book is called the ActiveBook. You will need to use the ActiveBook throughout the course.

ActiveBook

The ActiveBook is interactive.

▶ It contains examples of real-life publications.

▶ It provides activities for you to do.

▶ You can search the ActiveBook by topic.

▶ It makes learning more interesting.

Look for this symbol 🔅. Wherever you see it, you can click on it to access a digital resource.

▶▶Activity 1.1

Try it now.

1 **Click on the ActiveBook tab and open the ActiveBook.**

2 **Move around the ActiveBook and check out different links.**

3 **Then find your way back to this page.**

Can I do this?

This is a very useful feature of the ActiveBook. It will help you check you have the necessary skills as you work through the book. It gives you two options:

▶ '**Tell me**' takes you step-by-step through a task on the computer.

▶ '**Test me**' checks that you know how to do the task.

This is an extract from *Can I do this?* in Chapter 10.

You can also use the Skills list on pages 176–81 to check your skills.

Can I do this?

Using email tools, make sure you can:

Receive an email

Reply to an email

Send an email

Send an attachment

▸▸Activity 1.2

1　Click on one of the tasks listed in the *Can I do this?* box on the previous page.

2　If you think you know how to do the task already, choose 'Test me'. If you are not sure how to do this, choose 'Tell me'.

3　Now do the same with the other tasks.

Activities

Sometimes you will do activities on your own, at other times you will be asked to work in a pair or a group.

Many of the activities make use of digital resources provided on the ActiveBook. Click on the ▸ symbol to find the digital resources.

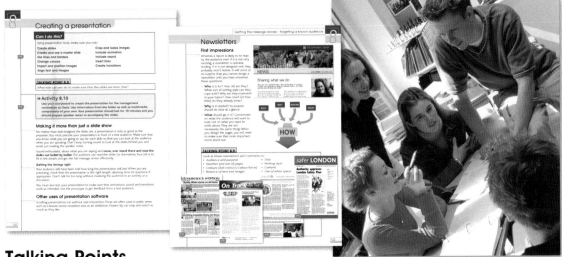

Talking Points

Talking Points allow time for discussion with others in your group. It is very important to share your ideas and find out what other people think. This can only make your work better! Here is the first Talking Point …

TALKING POINT 1.1

You have now looked at some of the features of the ActiveBook. What are the advantages of having an ActiveBook as well as a printed book?

Tackling THE PROJECT

The final page in most chapters is called **Tackling THE PROJECT.** In these pages you will practise the skills you need for the SPB.

What else is on the CD?

THE PROJECT

THE PROJECT gives you the chance to practise for the SPB.

You do THE PROJECT in small chunks, whereas the SPB is done in a block at the end of the course.

THE PROJECT is a mini website, just like a real Unit 1 SPB. It will help you to become familiar with the layout of the SPB.

You don't have to produce a complete project plan for THE PROJECT because you are told when to tackle each section. For the SPB, you will need to plan your work carefully so that you complete everything within the time allowed.

▸▸Activity 1.3

THE PROJECT is just like a website with links to various materials you will need. Click on THE PROJECT tab and have a look at THE PROJECT brief. Don't try to make a start just yet! Check out the different materials that are on the site.

The Digimodules

Your teacher will introduce each chapter using a digimodule. This is a multimedia presentation which introduces the topic of each chapter.

The other tabs

▸ **Go Online:** This takes you directly to the Edexcel DiDA course website.

▸ **Help:** This tab explains how to use the ActiveBook.

Zoom tools

You can zoom in on areas of the ActiveBook to make them easier to look at. Click anywhere on the page to enlarge that area. Clicking again will take you back to the full page view.

When you have zoomed in on an area, you can click the left or right arrow to scroll from one zoom area to the next. Clicking the magnifying glass icon or clicking anywhere on the page will take you back to the full page view.

What do you need to learn?

What you need to learn is explained in the specification. This page gives you an overview.

1 What you need to learn

DiDA is all about applying your ICT skills to communicate information as effectively as possible.

First you will need to gather the information you need. You will learn how to find, select and store information that is already available. You will also learn how to gather new information yourself. This will include doing surveys and interviews and using cameras and other equipment.

You will practise good design techniques so you can present your information well. You will learn how to make use of feedback so your publications are fit for audience and purpose.

You will learn how to design, develop and test an eportfolio.

TALKING POINT 1.2

Look at section 1 of the specification, 'What you need to learn'. How much of this do you know already?

2 Managing your project

You need to plan your project carefully for it to be successful. You will learn how to produce a project plan and use it to check on your progress and meet your deadlines.

You will also learn how to carry out a review of a project. This will help you to evaluate how well you have done.

TALKING POINT 1.3

Look at section 2 of the specification, 'Managing your Project'. Why is it so important?

3 The ICT skills you will need

These sections include all the ICT skills you will need and the types of software you should be able to use.

▶▶ Activity 1.4

Look at the ICT skills list in the specification now and see what you know already. You may surprise yourself!

... and the rest

This rest of the specification for Unit 1 is meant for teachers and moderators.

What are standard ways of working?

DiDA is all about using ICT effectively. Section 2.3 of the specification is called *Standard Ways of Working* and deals with things to think about when working with computers. These include working safely and managing your files.

How do you work safely?

You should already know some of the rules about working safely. It is easy to get information on how to reduce health and safety risks in your workspace.

Bad and good habits

▸▸Activity 1.5

1 **Open the questionnaire below. Answer the questions.**
2 **What bad habits do you have when you use a computer? Decide what action you will take.**
3 **After a week, check to see if you are still working safely.**

Working safely questionnaire

file:///Users/robbriggs/Desktop/Working%20safely%20questionnaire.htm

London Eye   Welcome to ...   QuarkStore   Apple   .Mac   Amazon   eBay   Yahoo!   News ▾

Working safely questionnaire

Is this you?		What can you do about it?	Planned action	Follow up
Do you work at a computer for long periods?	☐	Take regular breaks – at least 15 minutes away from the computer every two hours	☐	☐
		Take a short break from typing and looking at the screen every 10-15 minutes	☐	☐
Do you sit for long periods in one position?	☐	Take regular breaks. Get up and move around	☐	☐
		Use an adjustable swivel chair	☐	☐
		Move the printer away so that you have to get up to reach it	☐	☐
Do you lean forward rather than use the chair backrest?	☐	Check position of back and seat of chair. Use the backrest for support	☐	☐
		Make sure there is enough leg room	☐	☐
		Check readability of screen	☐	☐
		Get an eye test	☐	☐
Do you sit with your body twisted?	☐	Make sure there is enough leg room	☐	☐
		Use a swivel chair	☐	☐
		Arrange workspace in a U shape	☐	☐

It won't happen to me!

Have you ever lost important ICT work and had to do it all again? Do you think that it won't happen to you?

Take a look at this pie chart showing the main reasons people lose work.

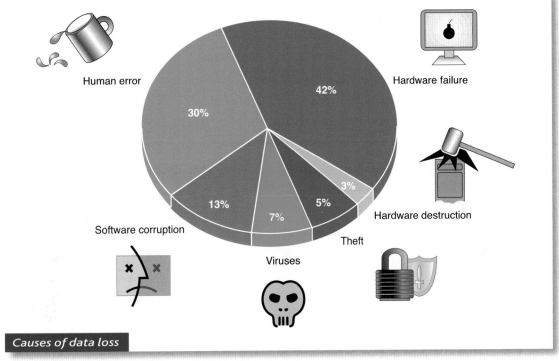

Human error 30%

Hardware failure 42%

Software corruption 13%

Viruses 7%

Theft 5%

Hardware destruction 3%

Causes of data loss

Let's look at some of these in more detail and see what you can do to protect your work.

Viruses

Viruses are programs that run without you realising it. Why do people write them? To cause trouble, for fun, for revenge or perhaps for a challenge.

Viruses can damage or destroy your files. Anti-virus software is very good at preventing viruses from attacking your system. But new viruses appear all the time so you must keep it up to date.

System destruction

Hardware, and everything stored on it, can be destroyed or damaged by flood, power surge, fire, lightning or equipment failure.

Hardware failure and software corruption

However hard you try, things can still go wrong. Hardware and software can let you down and work can be lost.

Human error

When you are working under pressure it is very easy to make mistakes. Around a third of all data loss is our own fault.

What can you do about it?

Here are some tips to help you avoid losing your work.

Saving your work

▶ Whenever you start a new document, save it **immediately** with the correct file name and in the correct location.

▶ Think before you click on the 'Save' icon. Do you want to overwrite the existing file or do you need to save the work under a new filename?

▶ Stop and read the dialogue boxes that appear.

▶ Save your work at regular intervals – or set up your PC so that it does this automatically.

▶ Keep a record of important filenames and locations.

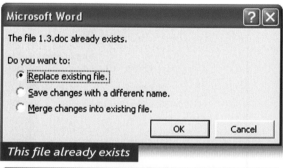

This file already exists

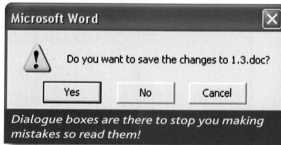

Dialogue boxes are there to stop you making mistakes so read them!

Backup

▶ Make backup copies of all work you want to keep. It is no good simply making a copy on the same hard disk as the original file. Make a copy somewhere else.

▶ Never overwrite your only backup with the next version. If the system fails in the middle of the backup procedure you will lose everything!

Protecting your work

▶ Use passwords to protect your system or folders.

▶ Use anti-virus software. Make use of automatic updates.

▶ Don't download files from unknown sources. Viruses are often sent out as attachments to emails. Don't open attachments from unknown sources. Delete them and empty the recycle bin.

▶ Avoid sharing portable devices such as memory sticks.

TALKING POINT 1.4

Discuss what measures are taken in your centre to keep ICT work safe.

How should you manage your work?

Can I do this?

Using software such as Windows Explorer, make sure you can:

Create folders and subfolders

Move around a folder structure

Find a file by searching

Save a file in a folder or subfolder

Copy a file or folder

Move a file or folder

Delete a file or folder

Use passwords for logon and folders

Change a file or folder name

Clearing the clutter

'I can't find my file.'

Do you recognise the situation in the cartoon? Remember, organising and storing your work is just as important as creating exciting publications.

How should you go about it?

First, clear the clutter! Get rid of unwanted files. It is useful to keep one or two draft versions of each piece of work while you are doing DiDA. However, you do not need to save lots of different versions.

Second, create a clear folder structure. Make a folder for each section of your work and give it a sensible name.

What folder structure should you use?

Some people have folders for different types of publications – letters, memos, presentations, etc. Others create a folder for each of their projects, each of their clients or each of their hobbies. In the example below, the manager of a leisure centre has created a folder for each different area of his work.

Saving work to folders

▶▶Activity 1.6

Imagine you are setting up a new PC at home. Using a pencil and paper, draw out a folder structure for storing work on the new PC. First, create a folder for each person who will use the PC. Then add the subfolders that you think each person might find useful.

What should you call your folders?

As well as organising your folders in a logical way, you need to know what is in them. Make sure you use sensible folder names.

Keep them simple. Use abbreviations to keep folder names short but be careful that they make sense. For example, a subfolder called Final Publications could perhaps be shortened to FinPubs, but FP is too short and doesn't give enough information.

TALKING POINT 1.5

The table shows a list of folders on a PC. The list of contents is not in the correct order. Can you match the correct content to each folder?

Folder Name	Content of folder
CustServ	Accident book for each department and first aid manuals
XmasParty	Activities for a school induction week
Accidents	Bookings and posters for a Christmas Party
Holiday	Bookings and posters for a college party
Party	Files relating to homeless people in a city
Homeless	Flight and hotel confirmations for holiday in the Caribbean
Induction	Images and articles for the fan pages of a pop group website
FanPage	Letters to customers whose central heating is due for a service

Are all the folder names sensible? How would you improve the names?
Would you create any extra folders to make things easier to find?

▸▸Activity 1.7

1 Look at your own folders. Is everything stored in a logical way? Do the folder names make sense or do you need to open some of them to see what they are?

2 Rename any folders with unclear names. If you cannot remember how to do this, look again at *Can I do this?* on page 11 of the ActiveBook. Select 'Change a file or folder name' and then select 'Tell me'.

What should you call your files?

The rules are the same for files as for folders. Avoid general names such as letter1.doc, letter2.doc. Use names that give some idea of the content of the files.

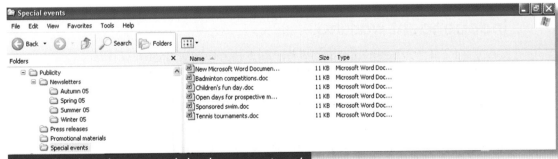

These files have been named clearly ... except one!

▸▸Activity 1.8

Look again at your user area. Do the file names make sense? Do you have the same files in different places? Or old versions of a document that you don't need any more?

Have a go at clearing your clutter now!

Looking for a file

▸▸Activity 1.9

1   Create a folder structure to store the work you will produce for the activities in this book. Don't worry about THE PROJECT – we will give you a structure for that.
Try this:
Create a folder called Unit 1.
⤷ Create subfolders for each chapter.
  ⤷ Create subfolders for drafts and final versions.

2   Do you think this will work for you? If not, come up with a different folder structure that you feel happy with. You can change the folder structure as you go along if you need to.

Independent working

Once a topic has been introduced by your teacher, you can work at your own pace using the ActiveBook.

Successful DiDA students will have the confidence to apply their ICT skills independently. However, this does not mean that you should work alone. You should always get feedback from others on what you are doing. It will make your work better.

You will get more marks in the SPB if you do most of your work independently. However, there are also marks for making use of feedback and for publications that show a good sense of audience and purpose.

Introducing SPBs

In the end, the final grade you get for Unit 1 will depend on the quality of work you produce for the SPB. **THE PROJECT** works in a similar way to an SPB.

▸▸ Activity 1.10

THE PROJECT brief is on your CD. Open it now. You will see that there is a menu to the left of the Introduction. Read the information below and try out the links.

Home	
Introduction	This section tells you the topic of **THE PROJECT** and gives you an overview of what you have to do.
Investigations	You will create a folder structure for **THE PROJECT** and begin to plan what you need to produce.
Gathering information	This section provides you with some sources of information for you to use in **THE PROJECT**. You will also plan where else to look for information.
Using a database	In this section you will design a form to enter data into a database, then add further records to an existing database.
Database reports	You will design and carry out searches in the database before creating reports that provide information.
Conducting a survey	In this section you will design a questionnaire and conduct your own survey about healthy eating. You will create a spreadsheet to analyse the data you find.
Survey report	Using your spreadsheet you will create charts for a report that presents the results of your survey.
Flyer	You will design a flyer to persuade students to attend your presentation.
Poster	You will design an eye-catching poster that attracts the attention of the target audience.
Leaflet	You will create a leaflet for junior school children to encourage them to eat more fruit.
Formal letter	This section provides you with two letters published in a newspaper. You will write a formal letter responding to one of them.
Information point	You will create an information point to give parents information about the healthy eating campaign.
Presentation	You will create a presentation on healthy eating.
Eportfolio	You need to design and build an eportfolio to present all of your work on **THE PROJECT**. This section explains what you must include and the file formats you can use.
Project review	Finally, you must review the work you have done and how well you have performed in this project. You will include the results of the review in your eportfolio.

Tackling THE PROJECT

P

By now you have already had look at THE PROJECT brief and made sure you know how to navigate through it (see Activities 1.3 and 1.10). Read the 'Home' and 'Introduction' sections of THE PROJECT brief again.

As you tackle each part of THE PROJECT, you will be producing lots of files. Not all of them will go into your eportfolio – you will choose exactly what to include later on. However, it's very important that you organise yourself from the beginning so that you can find the files when you want them.

Get organised!

Create a folder structure for your work on THE PROJECT like the one below. To do this:

1 Create a folder called 'The Project'.

2 Inside it create three folders called:

   'Gathering info'

   'Publications'

   'Review'.

3 Inside 'Gathering info' create three folders: 'Database', 'Survey' and 'Research'.

4 Inside 'Publications' create three folders: 'Attracting attention', 'Making info available', 'Known audience'.

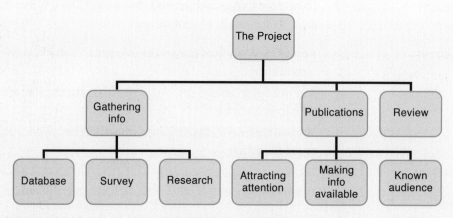

Later on you may decide to add more folders. For example, inside 'Attracting attention' you could add separate folders for your flyer and poster.

Producing an effective publication is all about making decisions. You need to decide:

Who the publication is aimed at (the target audience).

Why the publication is needed. Is it trying to give detailed information? Is it announcing an event?

Where the audience is. Are they people in your neighbourhood or scattered all over the place?

What your publication *must* include. What else do you want to add?

How to go about it. What type of publication is best? Will it be a poster, report, presentation, leaflet, web page or something else? What sort of language should you use?

In this chapter you will learn how to develop publications by deciding:

► *who the target audience is*
► *why the publication is needed*
► *where it is for*
► *what must go in it*
► *how you should go about it*

Who is it for?

Every publication is aimed at a group of people, called the target audience. The target audience may be very large or very small. Open the file and look at these examples.

TALKING POINT 2.1

This is a screen from an interactive story for children. What age group do you think the story is aimed at? Look at these questions to help you.

The Lost Boy   Screen title | Sound | On screen notes | | Close ✕
Back

It was a perfect day for going fishing. Gavin and Kate were on the deck of their dad's boat, *Kittiwake*. They could hear the chug of the engine, the cries of gulls, the slap of water against the boat's sides. The coast was out of sight, and the three of them were alone on the ocean.

TALKING POINT 2.2

Now look at this notice that is displayed at an ice rink.
▶ *Why is it needed?*
▶ *Who is the target audience?*
▶ *Will it catch the attention of the audience?*
▶ *Would you stop and read it? Why or why not?*

Ice Rink Rules

1 Please skate in a clockwise direction around the ice rink. Do not skate across the ice. Do not go back against the flow of skaters.
2 Any medical condition that may be affected by skating must be reported to a steward before skating.
3 Skates must be removed before leaving the rubber mats around the ice rink.
4 Climbing on the barriers around the rink is not permitted.

In order to produce an effective publication, you need to know who your target audience is. Here are some questions that will help you to understand your target audience:

- ▶ Is the audience one person or a group of people?
- ▶ Are they named individuals or a random group?
- ▶ Are they in a particular area or spread out?
- ▶ Are they a particular age or mixed ages?
- ▶ Do they know anything about the subject of the publication?
- ▶ How much do they know already?
- ▶ Will they be looking for the information or do you need to attract their attention?
- ▶ How will they access the information?

Once you are clear about your target audience, you will know which types of publication are suitable and which are not.

TALKING POINT 2.3

Look at the publications below. For each one, ask the questions above. Who is the likely audience for each?

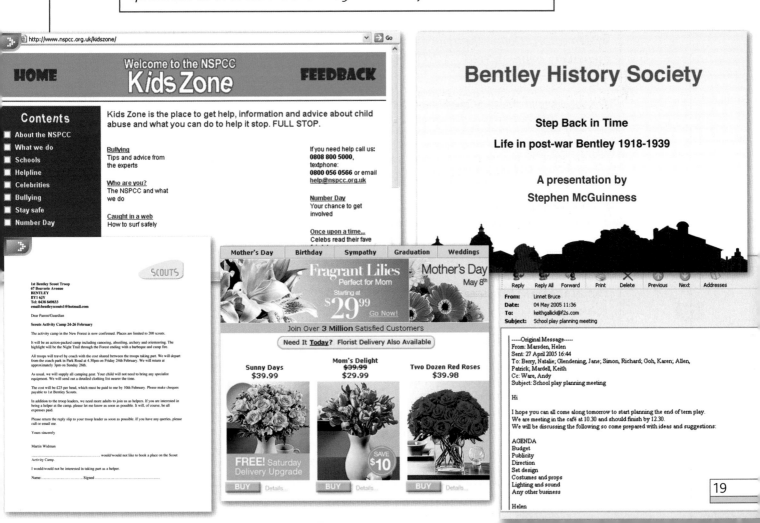

Why is it needed?

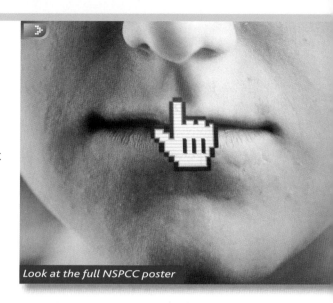

Look at the full NSPCC poster

Once you know who a publication is for, you need to think about why it is needed.

There are a number of reasons why you might want to present information to a target audience.

Do you want to attract attention?

Posters are a good way of catching people's attention.

TALKING POINT 2.4

What makes the NSPCC poster above catch people's attention? Look at these questions to help you.

Do you want to inform people?

The letter from the scout leader on page 19 shows how a letter can give clear and accurate information.

TALKING POINT 2.5

Think of publications that are designed to give people information. Divide them into three categories:
- ▶ *usually paper-based* ▶ *usually electronic* ▶ *can be either.*

Do you want to collect data?

You may want to collect information from people, rather than giving them information.

Questionnaires are often used in this situation.

TALKING POINT 2.6

A questionnaire is an example of a publication used to gather data. Look at this questionnaire. Who is the audience? Why do you think it is needed?

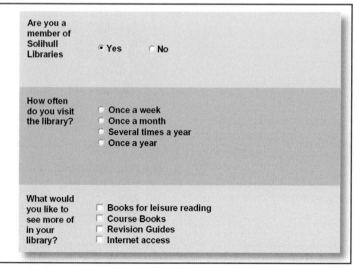

Do you want to persuade people?

Adverts are an obvious example of publications that try to persuade us to buy something.

Charities and political campaigns also use publications to try to persuade people to support them.

TALKING POINT 2.7

Imagine you have been asked to produce a poster advertising a disco for 14–16 year olds in aid of Children in Need.
Who is your target audience? Why do you need a poster? What are you trying to persuade them to do? How might you try to persuade them to do this?

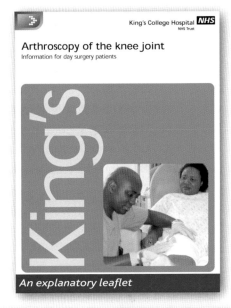

An explanatory leaflet

Do you want explain something?

Sometimes you need to explain something in detail. This might mean you have to use a lot of text. You can break text up with headings, paragraphs and lists to make it easier to read. Diagrams often help to make information clearer.

Do you want to impress someone?

A job application letter or a CV that is badly presented is not likely to lead to an interview.

TALKING POINT 2.8

Look at these two drafts of a CV.
▶ *Who is the intended audience?*
▶ *Which draft is more fit for purpose?*
▶ *Why?*

▶▶Activity 2.1

1 In groups, collect some examples of publications, both paper-based and on screen.
2 Identify the audience and purpose of each.
3 Try to identify one good feature and one that could be improved.

Where and what?

Where is the audience?

All in one room?

If the audience is gathered in one room, such as for a training day, a spoken presentation with handouts is an often a good choice.

Passing through?

Often your target audience will be passing through a location, such as a reception area or a library. However, you do not know exactly who they are.

Posters might attract their attention; an information point might help them find their way around. Or they might pick up a leaflet.

All over the place, but you know how to contact them?

If you have contact details, you can send letters, reports or emails. If you decide to put the information on a website, you will still need to contact your audience to let them know where to find it.

Anyone, anywhere?

A website is a good way of reaching a wide audience, but people need to have internet access. The website also needs to be easy to find.

You can try to reach a wide audience by sending out flyers or leaflets through the post to people who have not asked for it. This is often called 'junk mail' and people may ignore it.

Some companies use email to do the same thing. This is known as 'spam'.

TALKING POINT 2.9

What do you think about sending information to people when they have not asked for it? Why do companies do it? What problems does it cause? What items are you most likely to stop and look at?

What must go in it?

Once you know who, why and where, you can think about what information is needed. This is covered in detail in Chapter 3. At the moment, you just need to know enough to choose the right type of publication.

How do you go about it?

Think carefully before you start to produce a publication. Memorise this diagram and check that you understand it.

| TALKING POINT 2.10 |

What does this diagram show? What do you think each word refers to?

WHO WHY WHERE WHAT

HOW

Think carefully before you decide how

Screen vs paper

Should the publication be available on screen or on paper?

▶ **Paper:** If there is a lot of text, people tend to read it more carefully on paper. If it will be sent by post or handed out, it needs to be on paper.

▶ **Screen:** Digital publications are often cheaper and can be more flexible. Presentations and websites are good examples. They can include multimedia components, such as animations. They can also be easily updated.

Screen vs paper

| TALKING POINT 2.11 |

The Students' ActiveBook Pack has a printed book and an onscreen ActiveBook. When will it be most useful to use the ActiveBook? When will it be most useful to use the printed book?

Choosing the right type of publication

Different publications suit different purposes. Here are some examples.

Purpose	Examples of publications
To attract attention	Posters
	Flyers
To make information available	Leaflets
	Websites
	Information points
To target individuals or groups	Presentations
	Letters
	Reports
	Newsletters

TALKING POINT 2.12

Look at the posters below and discuss whether they are fit for purpose.

▶ *Why has each of the posters been produced? (purpose)*

▶ *Who is the target audience for each poster?*

▶ *How does each poster attract attention?*

▶ *Is the information clearly presented?*

▶ *Which poster do you think does its job best? Why?*

▶▶Activity 2.2

1 Search the internet for some websites about healthy eating.

2 Write down answers to each of these questions:

▶ Who is the website aimed at?

▶ What is it trying to do – attract attention, persuade, provide information?

▶ Do you think the website does the job it sets out to do? Is it fit for purpose?

▶▶Activity 2.3

Work with another student from your group. Match an appropriate publication with each audience and purpose.

Decide whether the aim of each publication is to:

a) attract attention

b) make information available

c) target individuals or groups.

Audience and purpose	Publication	Aim
Informing a customer that his central heating is due for a service		
Informing office staff of the date of a Christmas party		
Informing your supervisor of the common types of accidents that occur in the office		
Persuading people to take a holiday in the Caribbean		
Advertising a party in the college refectory		
Informing readers about the problems faced by homeless people in a city		
Providing information to fans of a pop group, giving up-to-date details of their tour dates		
Giving information on a company to new employees at an induction		
Sending a copy of some instructions to a technician who needs the information immediately		

Different publications are designed for different audiences

How do you choose the style?

You can create a completely different impression by changing the language you use or the way you present information.

Choosing a writing style

The informal style you use for an email to a friend is very different from the formal style used in a business letter.

When writing for young children you need to write more simply than you would for adults. Always choose a style that suits the audience and purpose.

▸▸Activity 2.4

Work in pairs. The sentences on the left are written for an adult audience. Can you rewrite them so that children between 6 and 8 years old will understand?

Adults' version	Children's version
The powder may have settled during transport and may need to be loosened.	Give the box a good shake!
Do not attempt to leave the bus while it is in motion.	
The glass door was fractured by the impact of the football.	
Bananas are particularly beneficial for athletes undertaking endurance events.	
You are politely requested not to cause disturbance when leaving the cinema.	

Choosing a presentation style

Different publications use different fonts, colours and layouts depending on the audience and purpose of the publication. You need to think carefully about the style you will use. What are you trying to achieve? Should the publication attract attention, appeal to children, look professional, impress someone?

▸▸Activity 2.5

Visit the BBC website. Use the worksheet to help you to compare two different parts of the BBC site.

TALKING POINT 2.13

Compare these two versions of Martin's letter.
▸ *What impression does each give?*
▸ *Which one is most suitable for the intended audience and purpose?*

Design and prototyping

Here are some top tips from successful DiDA students:

Things you can do to help yourself:

'Design your publication before you create it. I prefer to start with a blank sheet of paper, a pencil and a rubber. I sketch out what I think the publication should look like.'

'Keep reminding yourself of the audience and purpose.'

'Check that your publication matches your design.'

'Don't expect to get it right first time. Produce a prototype – a draft version – for testing.'

'Proofread it carefully. Use the spellchecker, but don't rely on it. It won't pick up all the mistakes.'

'Try reading it aloud. This will show up any clumsy sections, or things that don't make sense.'

Things other people can help you with:

'Ask people to comment on your prototypes. You should ask test users who are similar to the target audience, other students in your group and your teacher.'

'I find it works best if you give test users a questionnaire or checklist.'

'Tell everyone who looks at your work that you want the truth.'

'If other students ask you to test or review work, give it proper time and attention. Be helpful to them and they will help you in return.'

TALKING POINT 2.14

Why is it important to produce prototypes and get feedback? Why is it important to ask test users, other students and your teacher? Do you think they will tell you different things?

Giving feedback to others is an important skill that you will need to use many times during your DiDA course. Remember to tell the truth, but without being rude or unkind. You should mention all the good features as well as those that need improving.

▸▸Activity 2.6

1 In pairs, discuss what questions you need to ask yourself when giving feedback on a publication. Produce a questionnaire for test users of any publication.
2 Ask another student to test your questionnaire by using it to give feedback on a publication. They could use one of the publications collected in Activity 2.1.
3 Ask for comments on your questionnaire. Make improvements.

The production cycle

This diagram shows the production cycle. Keep it in mind every time you develop a publication. Keep going back to the design stage until you have a publication that is fit for purpose.

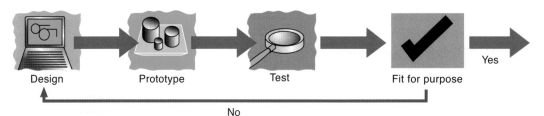

Design   Prototype   Test   Fit for purpose   Yes

No

TALKING POINT 2.15

Can you explain the production cycle to others in your group? What do you think might go wrong at each stage? Think about how much time you have and who you will ask to test your publication.

Keeping records of feedback

You need to keep careful records of the feedback you receive and changes you make as a result. When you do the SPB, the moderator will want to see evidence of how you made use of feedback.

Later in this book you will be given some checklists to help you collect feedback from test users. Keep the completed checklists in a safe place, especially if they are handwritten.

You can summarise the feedback from others in a document. For example, Charlotte is a DiDA student who asked her teacher for feedback on a questionnaire.

<u>Comments on my questionnaire</u>

Mrs Jones is my ICT teacher. I showed her my first attempt at the questionnaire. She liked most of the questions I asked but thought that Question 1 was not needed. She suggested that I make Question 2 simpler and that I should add another answer to Question 4b for saving energy. She said that people would not know what the survey was about so I should write an introduction. She also noticed the word 'warning' should be 'warming' in question 2 and said I should not rely on the spellchecker so much. The rest of her comments were about layout – the boxes and numbers need to be lined up.

Charlotte's summary of feedback from Mrs Jones

Annotation

Comments can be added using text boxes or comments/notes, if your software has these features. Here is the prototype of the questionnaire that Charlotte showed to Mrs Jones. She annotated it to show the feedback. It is easy to see how Charlotte revised her questionnaire after getting the feedback.

Alternative energy

Needs an introduction expla... what survey is for.

1a. Are you under the age of 21?   YES   NO

Don't need questions 1a,b unnecessary.

Can you make question 2 a bit clearer?

If answer is no finish here.

1b. Please state your age ....

2. On a scale of 1-5 how aware are you of the problems with global warning (1 being unaware, 5 being very aware)

1   2   3   4   5

Line the numbers up with the boxes

3. On a scale of 1-5 how concerned are you about these problems?

1   2   3   4   5

Line these boxes up with the ones in question 2

4a. Do you actively do anything to try and help these problems?

YES   NO

4b. If you answered YES to 4a please tick the category that your type of help fits into:

Alternative energy survey

This questionnaire is for people aged between 14 and 21. I have designed this questionnaire to find out how much teenagers know about the energy problems in the world today. My aim is also to find out whether you are doing anything to help the energy problem, or if not whether you would be willing to start trying. Thank you for your time!

1. On a scale of 1-5 how aware are you of problems caused by global warming (1 being unaware, 5 being very aware)

1   2   3   4   5

2. On a scale of 1-5 how concerned are you about these problems?

1   2   3   4   5

3a. Do you actively do anything to try and help these problems?

YES   NO

3b. If you answered YES to 4a please tick the category that your type of help fits into:

Do you think Mrs Jones will like the revised version?

▸▸ Activity 2.7

Look again at the CV you discussed in Talking Point 2.8. Using word processing tools, make suggestions about how it could be improved using comments/notes or text boxes.

James Peter Edwards
19 Lordsbridge Raod
STANEGATE
NP20 4BD
Telephone: 0220 993 428
Email: james@lordsbridge.co.uk

DOB   11 August 1987

Nationality: British

Marital status: Single

Driving licence   Hold full motor vehicle drivving licence

Education and Qualifications:

2002–05:   Stanegate College of Further Education, Stanegate
                BTEC National Diploma in Sport and Exercise Science

1998 – 2002:   Stanegate Community College, Stanegate
10 GCSE subjects including Maths, English, French, Combined Science all at Grade C
Member of the College 1st XI soccer team - Have also represented the College in
                County swimming galas and soccer tournaments.

Work experience

September 2005:   Trainee leisure manager at the Oasis Leisure Centre – doing some
                swimming instruction as well

Aug 02:   Worked at the Oasis Leisure Centre during the school holidays as
                a general dogsbody.

Nov 2001:   Two weeks at the Oasis Leisure Centre, working as a sports
                assistant. I organised a fab event for Children in Need.

Leisure activities and interests:

Mountain bikeing, soccer, swimming.

Tackling THE PROJECT

P

When you do the real SPB you will have to plan your work very carefully. Although **THE PROJECT** brief is a lot like a real SPB, you will do the work in stages as you work through the book – so a lot of the planning is done for you!

Now it is time to start thinking about the publications you are going to produce. Before you make a start on your publications, you need to think carefully about these questions:

▶ **Who** is the target audience?

▶ **Why** is it needed?

▶ **Where** is it for?

▶ **What** must go in it?

▶ **How** will you go about it?

Follow the instructions in the 'Investigations' section of **THE PROJECT** brief. Make sure you read the whole of **THE PROJECT** brief.

Make sure you keep your diagrams somewhere safe.

3 Making use of information sources

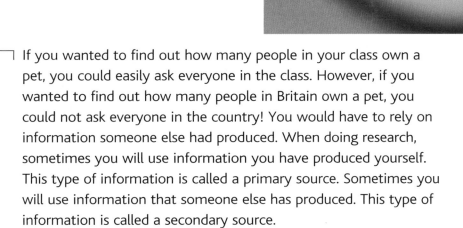

If you wanted to find out how many people in your class own a pet, you could easily ask everyone in the class. However, if you wanted to find out how many people in Britain own a pet, you could not ask everyone in the country! You would have to rely on information someone else had produced. When doing research, sometimes you will use information you have produced yourself. This type of information is called a primary source. Sometimes you will use information that someone else has produced. This type of information is called a secondary source.

In this chapter, you will learn how to choose good sources and select suitable information. You will look at both primary and secondary sources. If you use someone else's information, you must acknowledge the source in your own publication and you may need to ask permission to use it.

In this chapter you will learn how to make use of information sources by:

► *deciding what information you need*
► *using secondary sources*
► *selecting suitable primary sources*
► *checking that information is accurate and unbiased*
► *recording and acknowledging sources of information*

What content is needed?

Content refers to the words and images that a publication contains. Before you can start looking for content for a publication you must know who it is for, why it is needed and where it will be used.

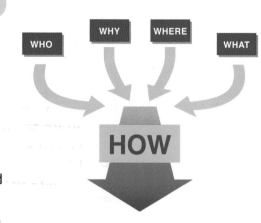

Using mind mapping to help you

A mind map is a useful way to bounce ideas around and make sure that you understand what is required. It also allows you to divide the work up into logical sections so that you can plan how to do it.

▶ **Start by putting your main idea in the centre.** It usually helps to use landscape format with all your ideas coming out from the centre.

▶ **Draw quickly without thinking too hard.** The idea of mind mapping is to think creatively. You should write down everything you can think of now. You can always change it later.

▶ **Use different colours** to make things stand out or to group different topics.

▶ **Show connections.** Use lines or arrows to show connections between the ideas.

▶ **Leave lots of space.** This will allow you to add things as you go along.

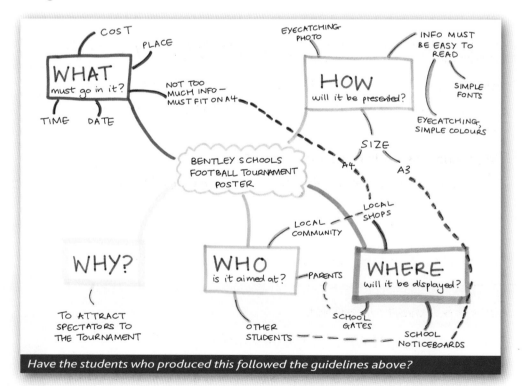

Have the students who produced this followed the guidelines above?

▶ Activity 3.1

Produce a mind map to show what content you will include in the information point for The Project. You should concentrate on one topic at a time and show connections between ideas. Make sure you read the relevant part of The Project brief before you start. Remember, your mind map does not have to be perfect. You can add to it as you go along.

Who is the audience?

An 'audience' is not just a group of people watching a performance. Anyone who sees a poster, reads a letter or report or uses an information point is referred to as 'the audience'. Every publication has an audience.

Different audiences need different approaches. For example, a poster on healthy eating for 6 year olds will be different from one aimed at 15 year olds.

The magistrate is likely to impose a detention and training order.

He's in a lot of trouble and may end up in jail.

Listen to a lawyer describe how he talks differently to different audiences

What does the audience need to know?

You need to think carefully about what information the audience needs. Ask yourself:

What does the audience know already?

If you are sure an audience already knows something, don't tell them again.

What must go in it?

What is the basic message of your publication? What information must you include?

How much detail is required?

You don't always need to include everything in one publication. For example, if you are doing a presentation, you might have handouts to go with it. You could include extra information in the handouts rather make the slides crowded with detail.

What style of presentation will work best?

The type of publication you make affects how you will present information. For example, on a poster, you won't have space for much text, but you will need an eye-catching image.

Also, make sure images are appropriate for the text. For example, don't put comic cartoons with very formal language.

Using ICT rooms

- No food or drink
- Place bags under chairs
- Check disks for viruses before use

The main points are set out clearly and briefly. The speaker will fill in the details.

What else do you need?

Once you know what must be included, you can think about what else you could use to help get the message across. For example:

- ▶ headings and sub-headings
- ▶ images
- ▶ sound or video.

What information do you have already?

You won't always need to start from scratch on a project. Sometimes you will already have some of the information you need.

TALKING POINT 3.1

Look at your mind map for the information point about healthy eating that you produced for Activity 3.1.

Draw up a list of the information that you need. Divide it into 'already have' and 'need to get'.

Information needed	
Already have	**Need to get**
Some images of different foods	Own photos for info point – healthy food?

Making life easier for yourself

Using the same information again

Text, images, video, digital photos, sound clips or anything you might use in a publication can be classed as 'information'.

When you are working on **THE PROJECT** or the SPB you will be able to use information more than once. For example, if you are planning handouts to go with a presentation, you may find that the same image can be used in both.

You could use a photo like this one in many publications for THE PROJECT.

> **TALKING POINT 3.2**
>
> *Look at the list of information you produced for the information point. Which items could also be used for other publications for* ***THE PROJECT***?

Planning your search for information

Planning always pays off; it will save you time and effort. For example, if you need to visit the library, it is best to plan what you need to find there so you don't have to go back again. See page 40 for an example of a plan for gathering information.

Keeping the information safe

Keep a record of where you get information from so that you can revisit a source when you need to.

How will you store all the information you find so that you can find things easily? Chapter 1, page 12, looks at file management. You will need to create a folder structure to store all the information for any publication or project. Don't forget to use file and folder names that make sense to you. Sometimes you will store the information itself and sometimes you will decide to store a link to it.

Keeping information safe

Information sources

How will you gather the information you need? Will you use information that is already available or will you create it yourself?

Secondary sources

If you use information that has been produced by someone else, you are using a secondary source. For example, you might:

▶ analyse data that someone else has collected

▶ use information from the internet

▶ use information from other places such as books, magazines, CDs, etc.

Often you will need to use a combination of different secondary sources.

Sources of information

Primary sources

Secondary sources will never give you everything you need. You will need to use primary sources as well. This means creating things yourself. For example:

▶ photographs, drawings or other images that you produce yourself

▶ surveys to gather data and produce charts

▶ interviews to find out opinions or to ask for information.

Remember to ask permission before you take a photo of someone or record what they are saying.

You will learn how to make effective use of primary sources in other parts of this book.

TALKING POINT 3.3

There are many ways of gathering information from primary sources. For example, you could use a tape recorder or a video camera to record an interview. How many more can you think of? Discuss the advantages and disadvantages of each.

Using secondary sources

Paper-based sources

These include:

- ▶ newspapers and magazines
- ▶ maps and drawings
- ▶ directories, such as Yellow Pages.
- ▶ books
- ▶ printed images

You will often find more information than you need. For example, if you find a long piece of text, only use the sections that are relevant.

> ### ▶▶ Activity 3.2
>
> **One way to identify the main points in a long piece of text is to highlight the first sentence of each paragraph. Reading the highlighted sentences should give you the main points of the article.**
>
> **Find an article on the subject of healthy eating and try out this method. Did you find it useful?**

Internet sources

Using a search engine

The internet is not like a library where staff can control what is available. Anyone can publish just about anything on the internet. This means that a lot of the information is unreliable. You can also end up with more information than you need.

Always think carefully about what you are trying to do and what information you need. Also think about how you use the search engine. For example, if you type the words 'healthy eating' into Google, you get over 71 million results or 'hits'. If you search pages from the UK only, you get nearer 6 million.

Refining the search

By adding keywords we can narrow down the search so that we get information that is more relevant.

> ### TALKING POINT 3.4
>
> *Think of a question related to healthy eating that you would like to know more about, for example 'How much fruit should I eat each day?'. What keywords could be added to 'healthy eating' to help find relevant information?*

▶Activity 3.3

1 Try searching for 'healthy eating' using Google. Then add the keywords that you discussed in Talking Point 3.4. If you find any sites that look useful, keep a record of them or bookmark them. Use the SOURCES file in 'Gathering information' section of THE PROJECT to keep a record of every source you use. Below is an example of how to fill this in.

2 Experiment with other keywords.

Secondary Sources – Websites				
Web address URL of useful page	Date last accessed	Website is about ...	Good for information on ...	I used this information in ... (which publication?)
eatwell.gov.uk eatwell.gov.uk/healthydiet/8tips/	14/3/06	Healthy eating	Tips for a healthy diet	Information point for parents

TALKING POINT 3.5

Compare your results with others in your group.

Why use the internet?

Don't assume that the internet is always better than using paper-based sources. There are advantages and disadvantages to each. Often it is best to use both, compare the results and then select the best information. Sometimes different sources will tell you different things. For example, you might find two different telephone numbers for the same business. You will need to investigate further to find out which is right.

▶Activity 3.4

Yellow Pages is a paper-based business telephone directory. There is an internet version called yell.com.

1 Find out the locations and phone numbers of pet shops in your area using each of these sources.

2 What are the advantages and disadvantages of each source?

Broadcast media

Radio and television programmes are useful secondary sources, especially if you need the latest information on current events.

Next time you watch the news on TV, look at how moving images, photos and diagrams are combined with sound. This can give television more impact than printed media.

Teletext and BBC interactive services also provide a wide range of information. This is useful for people who do not have access to the internet.

Unlike the internet, most of the content on broadcast media is independently checked.

Avoiding plagiarism

Plagiarism means presenting someone else's information or ideas as if they were your own. This is illegal. You must acknowledge the source of any information you use. You can avoid plagiarism by clearly acknowledging the source of the information.

DiDA students should understand that plagiarism is not allowed. We encourage you to make use of secondary sources, but you must show where you got the information from. You must also ask permission if necessary. Follow these rules and you will avoid problems.

The rules

You must work independently and produce your own work.

If you copy from secondary sources, you must show clearly where the information has come from.

If you summarise information from a source in your own words, you must still acknowledge it.

Always ask permission to use someone else's work.

You must not use another student's work under any circumstances.

TALKING POINT 3.6

What does 'plagiarism' mean? Why is it wrong? What is an 'acknowledgement'? Look at the back of your Student's Book and find the acknowledgements. What do they acknowledge?

Capturing information

Getting organised

Now it is time to think about where you will get information. You may find it helpful to draw up a table. This will help you plan where to look and keep a record of permissions. Here is an example:

Plan for gathering information			
Publication: Information Point for the project on healthy eating			
What I need	**Primary or secondary?**	**Where?**	**Notes on permission**
Photos of fruit & veg	Primary	Local fruit & veg shop Take photos with digital camera.	Ask permission.
Tips on healthy eating	Secondary	Internet search T.V. documentary	Record and acknowledge source.

▶▶Activity 3.5

Fill in the table for the information point on healthy eating for THE PROJECT. Use the list you created in Talking Point 3.1 to help you. Save the file in the correct folder. Use a sensible file name.

When you find the information you are looking for, you need to keep it somewhere safe. Store your information electronically. Make sure it is saved somewhere you can easily find it – remember to use sensible file and folder names! Record details of all the sources you use in your SOURCES file.

Capturing images

To capture an image you can:

- ► draw an image using drawing software
- ► draw an image by hand and scan it
- ► scan in an image from a paper-based resource
- ► scan in a photograph taken with an ordinary camera
- ► use a digital camera or a camera on a mobile phone.

Capturing paper-based images

You will probably use a scanner for this. Set it up carefully so that you get a good quality image without making the file size too big.

If you are using a secondary source, check with your teacher to make sure you are not breaking copyright laws. And remember to acknowledge all secondary sources!

TALKING POINT 3.7

What is meant by 'file size'? Why is it important to know the size of a file?

The image at the top has a file size of only 136KB, but the quality is poor. The image at the bottom is much better; it has a file size of 3.5MB

Capturing paper-based text

You can:

- ▶ type it in again
- ▶ scan it in.

If you scan the text you will not be able to edit it unless you use special software.

Whatever you do, remember that the text belongs to someone else. Do not use it without acknowledging the source, even if you rewrite it in your own words. Ask permission if necessary.

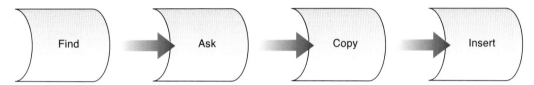

Find → Ask → Copy → Insert

▶▶ Activity 3.6

Open the file which contains this table:

Method	Primary, secondary or can be both?	Advantages	Disadvantages
Using drawing software			
Scanning in a drawing			
Scanning a printed image			
Scanning a photograph			
Using a digital camera			
Using a mobile phone camera			

Complete the table to show the advantages and disadvantages of each method. Note whether the source can be primary, secondary or both.

Can I do this?

Using suitable equipment, make sure you can:

Scan an image

Change the settings for a scan

Crop and resize scanned text and images

Use a digital camera

▸▸ Activity 3.7

1 **Open the folder of images provided to help you with The Project.**
   a) **Choose any image.**
   b) **Crop it – see what happens to the file size.**
   c) **Re-size it – see what happens to the file size.**

TALKING POINT 3.8

Discuss what is meant by 'resolution'.

Capturing information from the internet

There is so much information on the internet, you can easily end up with too much. Here are some tips to help you avoid information overload.

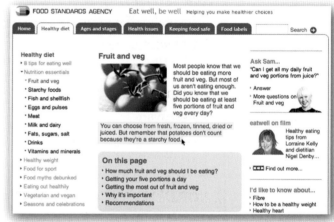

▶ Follow a plan – don't just browse.

▶ Don't print off too much information.

▶ Take handwritten notes for short pieces of information.

▶ Copy and paste longer sections or save a whole web page – but only if the material is really useful.

▶ Use bookmarks to help you keep track of where you have been.

▶ Keep a record of where you found each item in your SOURCES file.

Can I do this?

To capture information from the internet, you need to be able to:

Use an internet browser

Use a search engine

Refine searches using keywords and operators

Bookmark a page

Copy and paste a link

Copy and paste information

▶▶Activity 3.8

Look at this list of websites that are provided to help you with The Project.

1 Choose some short paragraphs and images that you think will be useful for any of your publications.

2 Copy and paste them into a document and make a note of what you might use them for.

3 Record the sources (including full URLs) so you can acknowledge them.

Using the internet safely

Don't:

► give out personal information like your name, address, or phone number when searching for information – some sites encourage you to do this

► open unknown email attachments. They can contain viruses which harm your computer.

Do:

► use only your log-in name and/or email address when sending email

► ask for help if you are worried about anything – just log off if you are unsure!

Capturing information from broadcast media

You may want to jot down notes from a radio or television programme. This is easier to do if you record the programme or if you access it online. Look at the BBC website to find out which programmes are available via the internet.

Freely available sources of information

Some websites allow you to use some or all of the resources, but you must read the terms and conditions of use to make sure you are using them correctly. Look at the list of these websites.

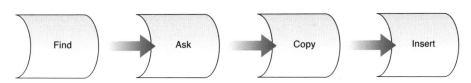

Find → Ask → Copy → Insert

Don't forget!

Checking it out

Don't take the information at face value. Check it out!

Much of the information on the internet is unreliable. If you want to be fairly sure that information is checked for accuracy, use official websites. Always compare what different sites say about a topic.

Whatever the source of the information, ask yourself:

▶ Is it reliable? Who said it, who produced it, where did they get it from?

▶ Do other sources say the same? If not, which is right?

▶ Is it up to date? Some types of data go out of date quickly.

▶ Is it unbiased? Why was it produced?

TALKING POINT 3.9

Information can be made to give out a particular message by the way it is presented.

Look at the chart. What is it meant to show?

Do you think it is misleading? Why?

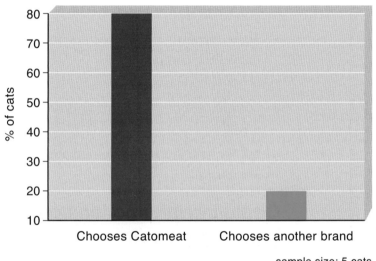

Chooses Catomeat   Chooses another brand

sample size: 5 cats

▶▶ Activity 3.9

There are lots of websites designed to help you to use information from the internet. One example is the Quick website. Your teacher may suggest other websites.

Explore one of these sites. Note down three things you can do to check that a website is reliable.

Acknowledging sources

When you use material that belongs to someone else, you must acknowledge where you got it from. Record details of sources in your SOURCES file as you use them. You will need to do this for your SPB so that you can include your sources in your eportfolio.

Much of the information will be copyright. You must check that you are not breaking the law when you use copyright sources. If you are unsure, ask your teacher.

Internet sources

Keep a record of:

- ▶ document title or description
- ▶ author (if possible)
- ▶ date of publication
- ▶ date accessed

- ▶ URL – this is the full web address for the *page* containing the information, not just the main website
- ▶ permission where necessary.

For example:

1 Andy Darvill, Solar Power is energy from the sun
   <http://www.darvill.clara.net/altenergy/solar.htm>
   (site accessed 24 May 2006)

Make sure that the addresses (URLs) you give are correct. It is best to copy the URL directly from the address window in the browser and paste it into your sources record sheet.

Paper-based sources

You should always include:

- ▶ author (if known)
- ▶ title of book, article, report, etc
- ▶ date of publication.

- ▶ publisher
- ▶ permission (where necessary)

For example:
Robert Dinwiddle, *Essential Computers: Creating Worksheets* (Dorling Kindersley, 2003)

Primary sources

If you interview someone, record their name and the date. If you present the results of a survey, record details of where and when the survey took place.

Tackling **The Project**

Look at the 'Gathering information' section of **The Project** website. You have already done quite a lot of this work. For your information point you have already:

▶ produced a mind map (see Activity 3.1)

▶ made a list of the information you already have and still need to gather (see Talking Point 3.1)

▶ made a table of all the information you need for the information point (see Activity 3.5).

You have also:

▶ thought about whether you will be able to re-use any of this information in your other publications (see Talking Point 3.2)

▶ found some sources of website information (see Activity 3.3) and photos (see Activity 3.7).

Now go through the same planning stages for your flyer, poster, leaflet and presentation. Remember to look back at the diagrams you produced for each of these publications in Chapter 2.

Add tables for each publication to the PLAN FOR GATHERING INFO document you started in Activity 3.5. Use this to plan your research for each publication. Make sure you keep the SOURCES file that you started in Activity 3.3 up to date with details of the information that you decide to use.

Collect your resources

Now collect as many of your resources as you can. Make sure you save all the information in the correct folders using sensible file names. Keep your SOURCES and PLAN FOR GATHERING INFO documents up to date.

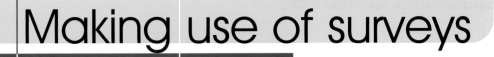

4 Making use of surveys

Questions! Questions! Surveys are all about asking questions to find out something useful. By asking lots of people the same questions, you can compare their answers and draw conclusions.

A good survey will:

▶ have simple questions

▶ find out the information that is needed

▶ ask the right people in the right way

▶ record people's answers so that they are easy to analyse.

Before computers existed, it was much more difficult to handle the data produced by surveys. ICT has made all the difference. Spreadsheets can be used to analyse surveys and to present the results using charts.

In this chapter you will learn how to make use of surveys by:

▶ *deciding what you want to find out*

▶ *deciding who to ask*

▶ *designing, testing and using a questionnaire*

▶ *analysing the results using spreadsheet tools*

Conducting a survey

Who do you ask?

When you conduct a survey, you need to decide very carefully who you want to ask and how many people you need to ask. But there is one survey that does things differently.

Let's ask everyone in the UK!

The Census is a survey of everyone living in the UK. It takes place every ten years. The 2001 Census gave us information about more than 58 million people. Everyone was asked the same questions at the same time. The results took ten months to analyse. Lots of organisations make use of the data.

Here is some data from the 2001 census:

Males	28.6 million
Females	30.2 million
Total population	**58.8 million**

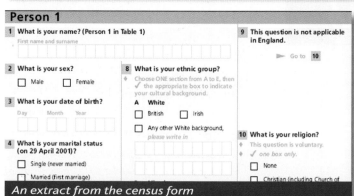

An extract from the census form

▶▶Activity 4.1

Look at the neighbourhood statistics section of the Census 2001 website. Enter your nearest town or your postcode and have a look at the results.

1   What is the total population of the area you have chosen?

2a Go to the *Health and Care* section. Find out the average life expectancy for men in your area. Is it higher or lower than the average for England and Wales?

2b What does this tell you about the health of people in your area?

Using a sample

Surveys cost time and money. If you cannot ask everyone you are interested in, you must use a sample. This means asking only some of the people.

Who should I include?

Is it possible to ask everyone?

If you wanted to find out what the members of a youth club think about moving the club to new premises, you might be able to ask all the members. You would not need to use a sample. If you wanted to know what teenagers in the UK think about smoking, you could not ask all the teenagers in the country! In that case, you would need a sample.

I can't ask everyone, so who should I ask?

You need to use a sample that will give a fair result. For example, if you want to find out what kind of music teenagers prefer, it is important to ask boys and girls in equal numbers.

How many people do I need to ask?

Your sample must be big enough to give reliable results. Asking just five people what they think about speed cameras would not be reliable. Asking 50 people might give you some useful data.

TALKING POINT 4.1

Can you explain what is meant by using a sample? What sort of things do you need to consider when choosing a sample?

Avoiding bias

You will get different survey results depending on who you ask.

Imagine you wanted to find out which type of music was most popular among teenagers. Your friends might all like similar music, so if you only asked them, your results would not represent the views of all teenagers. This is called bias. It would be better to ask a random selection of teenagers to avoid bias and get reliable results.

▸▸Activity 4.2

Look at this table. For each topic, decide which sample will give the most reliable results and explain why.

▸▸ Activity 4.3

This table shows some examples of samples that may be biased.

Survey to find out:	Sample	Possible bias	Should also include:
What people think about your art display	Your friends	They are more likely to say what you want them to say	Other teenagers and adults viewing the display
How much exercise people take in a week	Members of a leisure centre		
What people think about the proposed closure of the local cinema	People leaving the cinema		
How much people spend on Christmas presents	People on an email distribution list		
Whether people think university fees should be abolished	Students in a Students' Union Bar		

Complete the blank cells to show possible bias caused by the choice of people for the sample. How could you make each sample bigger to make the results less biased?

How many people should you ask?

Make sure your sample is big enough to produce useful results. The number of people you ask will also depend on how much time you have and how easy it is to contact the people you want to ask.

Where do you ask the questions?

You need to think about which method will work best for you. Here are some suggestions:

▶ send out a questionnaire by post

▶ send out a questionnaire using email

▶ interview people in the street

▶ interview people in a particular place, for example at school, at youth club

▶ interview people over the telephone.

Carrying out a survey

TALKING POINT 4.2

Look at the list of methods above. What are the advantages and disadvantages of each method of carrying out a survey?

Staying safe

You need to follow some basic rules when conducting a survey.

- ▶ Never approach people in the street on your own. Always work in pairs or a group.
- ▶ Never send out information to strangers that gives away your personal details.
- ▶ Always show your questions to your teacher before you use them.
- ▶ Discuss and agree other rules with your teacher before starting the survey.

Using questionnaires

A questionnaire can be used in two ways. It can be given to a person to fill in themselves or the researcher can ask the questions and write down the answers.

By using a questionnaire we can make sure that:

- ▶ the questions are carefully thought out in advance
- ▶ everyone is asked the same questions
- ▶ the answers are recorded in the same way.

HOW WELL DID OUR FACILITIES MEET WITH YOUR EXPECTATIONS?

	Excellent	Good	Average	Poor
Welcome upon arrival:	☐	☐	☐	☐
In your conference room:	☐	☐	☐	☐
In the Restaurant:	☐	☐	☐	☐
In the Conservatory Bar:	☐	☐	☐	☐
In the Keeper's Lodge:	☐	☐	☐	☐
Quality of food:	☐	☐	☐	☐
In your bedroom:	☐	☐	☐	☐
The golf course:	☐	☐	☐	☐
Golfing facilities:	☐	☐	☐	☐

An example of a questionnaire used to get feedback from hotel guests

TALKING POINT 4.3

Look at the questionnaire for hotel guests above. Imagine you are a guest who stays for just one night. Would you find it easy to fill in this questionnaire?

▶▶Activity 4.4

Collect some questionnaires from different sources, both printed and on screen. What are they for? Are they easy to fill in? Do the questions try to lead you to one particular answer?

Creating a questionnaire

What do you want to find out?

We are going to use an example to illustrate the things you need to think about when creating a questionnaire.

Imagine that the government is thinking about changing the rules for learning to drive. We asked a researcher what the issues might be. Listen to what he had to say.

How can you avoid influencing people?

You have to be careful not to influence how people respond to your questions.

If you want to know what people think the minimum age for driving should be, there are many ways of asking the question. Listen to these different ways of asking the same question:

- ► More accidents are caused by drivers under 25 than any other age group. What do you think the minimum age should be?

- ► What do you think the minimum age for taking a driving test should be?

- ► Most people think that 17 is too young to drive. Do you agree?

- ► Some people think that 17 is too young to drive. Do you agree?

TALKING POINT 4.4

Which of these questions might influence people's answers? How? What do you think is the best way to ask the question?

▶▶ Activity 4.5

You want to ask a question about how much fruit people should eat every day. How would you ask this?

1 In pairs, think of as many different ways of asking the question as you can.
2 With another pair, discuss how each way of asking the question might influence the answer.

Recording the answers

Keep it simple!

If you want to use a spreadsheet to analyse the data, you have to design your questionnaire in a special way. If you ask the question 'What do you think the minimum age for driving should be?' you might get many different answers.

If you limit the number of possible answers, the data is easier to analyse. You can do it by asking a question in this way:

What do you think the minimum age for driving should be?

lower than 17 ☐   17 ☐   18 ☐   19 ☐   20 ☐   21 ☐   higher ☐

You can then count up how many people chose each option.

Avoid information overload

Things get more complicated when you want to ask people the reasons for their opinions, for example: 'Why do you think the minimum driving age should be higher?'

The number of different answers to this question is endless. Also, each answer will be text. Text is not useful for calculations in a spreadsheet!

You need to limit the number of different options. The trick is to include a good range of different answers, for example:

- ▶ traffic is much faster now
- ▶ traffic is much busier now
- ▶ 17 is too young to be sensible
- ▶ other.

It is a good idea to include 'other' as you will never be able to include every possible option. However, when you test the questionnaire you can ask people to give any other reasons they have. You can then add more options to the final version if necessary.

TALKING POINT 4.5

Look at these questions taken from various questionnaires. Will any of these questions result in lots of different answers? Would it be suitable to give a list of options instead? If so, what options would you give?

Introducing your questionnaire

A questionnaire needs a heading and a simple explanation of what the survey is about. The layout must be clear and easy to use.

Developing the questionnaire

Here is the first draft of part of a questionnaire, called **Safe to Drive**. It aims to find out what people think about current laws and whether they should be changed. Someone has done some initial testing and added some feedback.

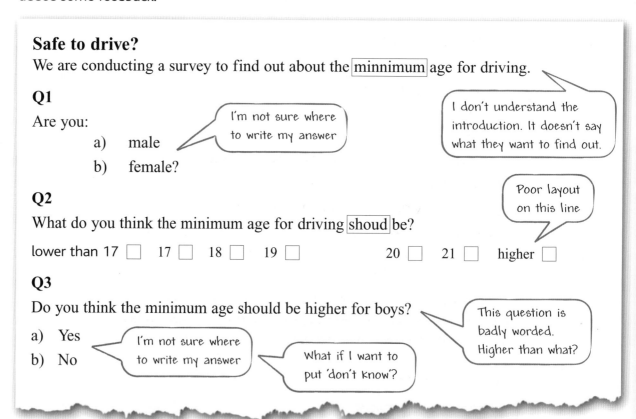

Can I do this?

Using word processing software, make sure you can:

Align text
Set tabs
Create and use a numbered list
Create tick boxes
Create and use a table
Insert page numbers

▸▸Activity 4.6a

Open the draft questionnaire. Save it as DRIVING QUESTIONNAIRE. Use the feedback given to make improvements.

When giving feedback on a questionnaire, ask yourself the following questions.

▶ Does this introduction make sense?

▶ Is it clear what the questionnaire is for?

▶ Are the questions clear?

▶ Are any of the questions worded so that they influence the answer?

▶ Is it clear where you should write the answers?

▶ Is there enough space for answers?

▶ Are there any spelling or grammar mistakes?

▶ What do you think of the choice of font styles and sizes?

▸▸Activity 4.6b

1 **Give your improved questionnaire to another group of students. Ask them to give you feedback, using the questions above to help them.**
2 **Use the feedback to improve the questionnaire.**

Building spreadsheets to analyse results

4

Can I do this?

Using spreadsheet tools, make sure you can:

Use formulae

Use SUM and AVERAGE functions

Use the IF function

Switch to and from formula view

Select areas for printing or charts

Create charts

Building a spreadsheet

Why choose spreadsheet software to analyse the survey results?

Spreadsheets allow you to calculate totals and percentages. They also allow you to produce charts that help to present the survey results.

How do you transfer the data from the questionnaires to the spreadsheet?

If you only want to find out how many people gave each response, you can use a simple tally chart like this one. You can then put the totals into your spreadsheet.

Q1 Are you male or female?

Males	JHT JHT JHT JHT JHT	25
Females	JHT JHT JHT JHT JHT IIII	29

This tally chart counts the answers to Question 1 of the 'Safe to Drive' questionnaire

TALKING POINT 4.8

This tally chart is more complicated. What does it show? What information does each section give you? How would you go about entering the information from the questionnaires into this tally chart?

Q3 Do you think the minimum age should be higher for boys than for girls?

	Males		Females		Total
Yes	II	2	JHT JHT III	13	15
No	JHT JHT JHT JHT	20	JHT JHT I	11	31
Don't know	III	3	JHT	5	8

This tally chart counts the answers to Question 3 of the 'Safe to Drive' questionnaire

Using and checking formulae

We are going to use a summary spreadsheet to analyse the data that we will collect from the **Safe to Drive** questionnaire. Before we enter the data from the actual survey we need to check that our formulae are correct and our spreadsheet works. We will enter some test data to do this.

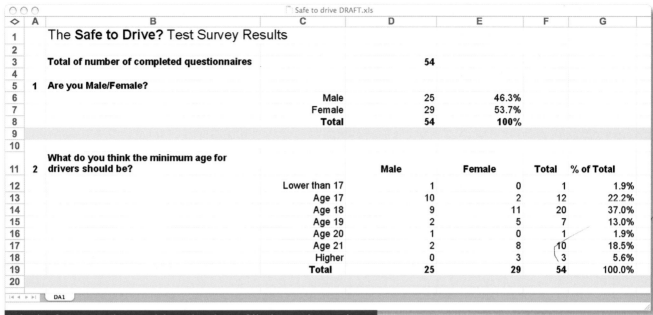

The 'Safe to Drive' spreadsheet has been filled in with test data

Which formulae should you use?

1 Open the spreadsheet in formula view.

F19 adds up the numbers in cells from F12 to F18. The total should be the same as the number of completed questionnaires in D3.

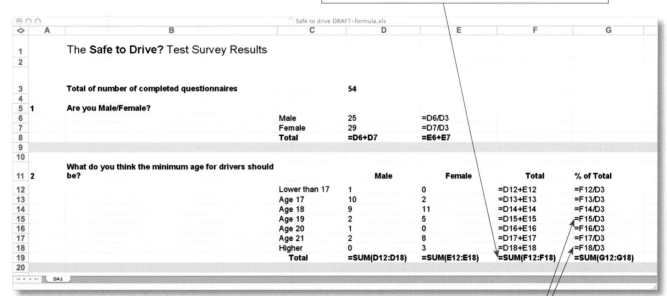

These formulae calculate the percentage of people who gave each answer. The total number of people who took part is stored in D3.

NOTE: These formulae will only display as percentages if the cells are formatted to percentage.

▸▸Activity 4.7

Open the draft Safe to Drive spreadsheet in formula view.

1 What does the formula in D8 do?
2 The value in D8 should be the same as a value in another cell. Which one?
3 Which other cells should have this value? Why?

TALKING POINT 4.9

Look at all of the formulae in the whole spreadsheet. What does each one do? Look at cell G22. What do you have to do to get it to display correctly?

Testing a spreadsheet

Just because you get results from a spreadsheet, it does not mean they are correct. Use a calculator to check that all the calculations are correct. If you get a different answer to the one in the spreadsheet, check the formula.

TALKING POINT 4.10

Open the Bentley High School Survey spreadsheet. What does the spreadsheet show?

▸▸Activity 4.8

Open the Bentley High School Survey spreadsheet and save it as BENTLEY SURVEY RESULTS.

1 The formula in cell D16 is wrong. It should display 298. Correct the formula.
2 There is an error in cell E22. Fix it.
3 The value in cell E35 should be 100%. What has gone wrong?

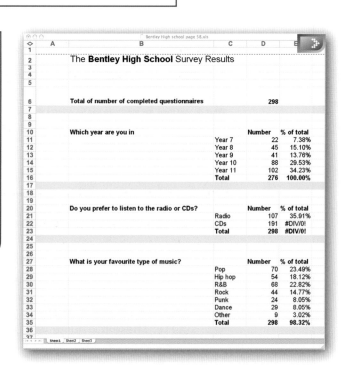

	The **Bentley High School** Survey Results			
	Total of number of completed questionnaires		298	
	Which year are you in		Number	% of total
		Year 7	22	7.38%
		Year 8	45	15.10%
		Year 9	41	13.76%
		Year 10	88	29.53%
		Year 11	102	34.23%
		Total	276	100.00%
	Do you prefer to listen to the radio or CDs?		Number	% of total
		Radio	107	35.91%
		CDs	191	#DIV/0!
		Total	298	#DIV/0!
	What is your favourite type of music?		Number	% of total
		Pop	70	23.49%
		Hip hop	54	18.12%
		R&B	68	22.82%
		Rock	44	14.77%
		Punk	24	8.05%
		Dance	29	8.05%
		Other	9	3.02%
		Total	298	98.32%

Final Safe to Drive spreadsheet

We tested the draft **Safe to Drive** spreadsheet using test data. Then we used the questionnaire to carry out a street survey. We interviewed 120 people. We recorded the data in the final spreadsheet.

	Safe to drive FINAL.xls					
A	B	C	D	E	F	G
1	The **Safe to Drive?** Final Survey Results					
2						
3	**Total of number of completed questionnaires**		**120**			
4						
5	**1 Are you Male/Female?**					
6		Male	58	48.3%		
7		Female	62	51.7%		
8		**Total**	**120**	**100%**		
9						
10						
11	**2 What do you think the minimum age for drivers should be?**		**Male**	**Female**	**Total**	**% of Total**
12		Lower than 17	16	0	16	13.3%
13		Age 17	24	26	50	41.7%
14		Age 18	7	7	14	11.7%
15		Age 19	8	12	20	16.7%
16		Age 20	2	5	7	5.8%
17		Age 21	1	9	10	8.3%
18		Higher	0	3	3	2.5%
19		**Total**	**58**	**62**	**120**	**100.0%**
20						
21	**3 Do you think the minimum age should be higher for boys than for girls?**		**Male**	**Female**	**Total**	**% of Total**
22		Yes	9	44	53	44.2%
23		No	34	15	49	40.8%
24		Don't know	15	3	18	15.0%
25		**Total**	**58**	**62**	**120**	**100.0%**
26						
27						
28						

Safe to Drive FINAL

Using charts to present results

Good charts are often the best way to get a message across. They can show the results of a survey at a glance.

We are going to create some charts using the results of the final **Safe to Drive** survey.

TALKING POINT 4.11

*This chart shows the answers to question 3 of the **Safe to Drive** survey. Does it show the answers given by males, females or both?*

Would the chart be clear to someone who has not seen the spreadsheet or the questionnaire? How would you improve it?

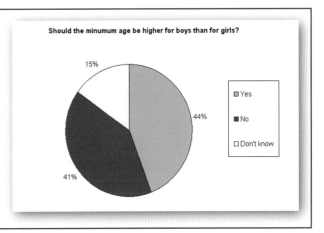

Should the minumum age be higher for boys than for girls?

15%
44%
41%

Yes
No
Don't know

Which type of chart should you use?

Column and bar charts

Column and bar charts are useful if you want to compare different answers to a survey question.

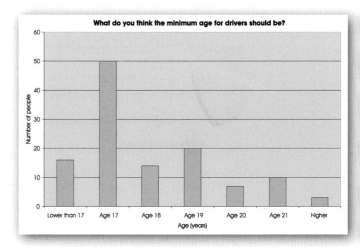

Pie charts

Pie charts are good for showing proportions or percentages, but they do not work well if there are too many items.

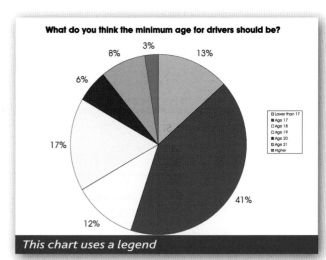

TALKING POINT 4.12

Open the chart showing the results of question 3 in the Bentley High School Music Survey. Is the information clear? How could this chart be improved?

Line graphs

Line graphs are used to show values that are always changing. For example, you could use a line graph to show the temperature over a year.

Survey responses do not have values that change. **Don't use line graphs for survey responses!**

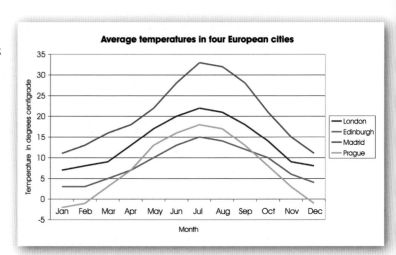

What will the chart be used for?

Charts in slide presentations

It is difficult to tell some paler colours apart on screen. Use bold colours for onscreen presentations.

In a presentation, the audience won't have much time to study the chart carefully. Make the chart as clear and simple as possible.

> **TALKING POINT 4.13**
>
> *Open the charts. If you were presenting the results of the **Safe to Drive** survey using a projector, which chart would you choose? Why?*

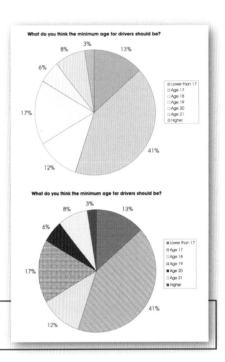

Charts in printed reports

If the chart is for a printed report, you can include more detail and explanation because readers will have time to take it all in.

Colour or black and white?

If a chart is printed in black and white, all colours become shades of grey. Some colours may come out as the same shade of grey.

> **TALKING POINT 4.14**
>
> *Which of these charts would you use in a printed report? Why?*

▶▶ Activity 4.9

Open the Bentley School Survey spreadsheet and experiment with different colours and patterns for the charts. Use black and white as well as colour. Use 'print preview' to check them.

Creating a chart

When creating a chart you need to ask yourself the following questions.

- ▶ Which type of chart is most appropriate?
- ▶ Is the scale sensible?
- ▶ Is it easy to read the values from the chart?
- ▶ Are the headings and labels clear? Do they give enough information to the reader?
- ▶ Are the colours clear?

You can use a chart wizard but remember that wizards are not magic. You need to customise them to get the chart you want.

Selecting the right data

People often include extra columns or rows when selecting the data. This results in charts that do not make sense.

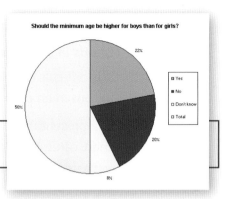

TALKING POINT 4.15

Look at this chart. What has gone wrong? How did it happen?

A meaningful title

This is the most important item. The title should clearly say what the chart shows or what question the chart answers. Without a clear title your audience cannot make sense of the chart.

Sensible axis labels

Make sure you label what each axis shows, for example, 'Number of people' and 'Response'. Labels help the audience to understand the chart.

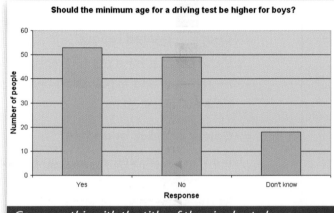

Compare this with the title of the pie chart above. Which is more helpful?

Gridlines and values

You should be able to read off the exact values of each part of the chart. You can insert gridlines and values to make this easier.

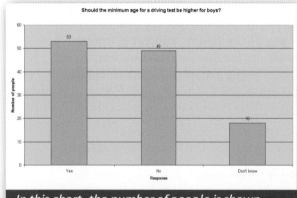

In this chart, the number of people is shown above each column.

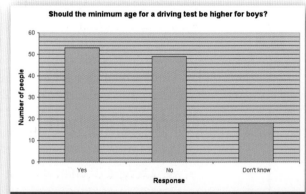

In this chart, extra gridlines make it easy to see the number of people.

▸▸Activity 4.10

Open the Bentley High School Survey spreadsheet. Add gridlines and values to the charts to make them clearer.

Legend or data labels

Your chart will include the row and column headings from your spreadsheet. They may be too long to use as horizontal data labels. Sometimes you can change the angle. Alternatively, you can use a legend.

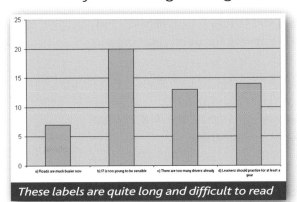

These labels are quite long and difficult to read

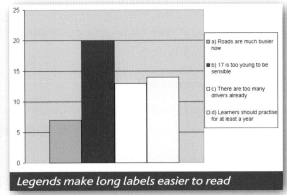

Legends make long labels easier to read

▸▸ Activity 4.11

1 Using the data from the **Safe to Drive FINAL** spreadsheet, produce charts to show:
  ▸ **what people think the minimum driving age should be (bar chart)**
  ▸ **whether people think the minimum driving age should be higher for boys than girls (pie chart)**
  Think carefully about the title, colours, labels, gridlines and legends.
2 **Get feedback and make improvements.**

Making comparisons

Sometimes you might want to find out if different groups behave differently or have different views. For example, in a questionnaire about TV viewing habits, you might want to find out if teenagers watch more or less television than people aged 20 to 30. For the **Safe to Drive** survey, you could produce a chart to compare male and female responses to the questions.

TALKING POINT 4.16

*What kind of chart would you use to compare male and female responses in the **Safe to Drive** survey? Why? Which data would you need to include?*

▸▸ Activity 4.12

Create a chart to compare male and female responses to question 3 of the Safe to Drive survey.

Tackling THE PROJECT

P

Questionnaire

First you are going to create your questionnaire. Read the first page of the 'Conducting a survey' section of the THE PROJECT. Now work through the activities described.

Save your final versions, prototypes and feedback. You will find out about how to produce acceptable file formats for your eportfolio in Chapter 9.

Spreadsheet

Read page 2 of the 'Conducting a survey' section of the THE PROJECT brief. Create and test your spreadsheet as described.

Survey

Now you have completed your questionnaire and spreadsheet, carry out your survey. **Remember the guidelines on staying safe on page 51**.

When your survey is complete, enter your data into your spreadsheet. Make sure you save the completed spreadsheet. You will learn how to create evidence of it for your eportfolio in Chapter 9.

Results

Open the 'Survey report' section of THE PROJECT brief. Produce the charts described. You will complete the rest of this section in Chapter 8, so make sure that you save your charts in your spreadsheet.

5 Making use of databases

More and more information is being stored about everything and everyone. Your school stores information, such as your date of birth, address and grades. Your doctor stores information about your medical history. The video shop stores information about which films you have rented, when they are due back and how much you owe in fines! A lot of this information will be stored in databases. This information is called data.

A database is a collection of data that is set up in a way that makes it easy to organise and search for information. Databases are much better for organising a range of data — including text, numbers, dates, times and images — than spreadsheets and other applications.

Databases can also be used to produce reports.

In this chapter you will learn to how to make use of databases by:

▶ *creating data entry forms that are easy to use*
▶ *entering data into a database*
▶ *sorting data in a database to make information clearer*
▶ *searching a database to find useful information*

Why use a database?

More and more data is generated all the time. Organisations need to be able to store, search and sort the data so that they can use it to help them.

Case study: The Boots Advantage Card

Many high street shops offer customers a loyalty card. Every time the customer buys something, the loyalty card is scanned and points are added. When customers have collected enough points, they can use them to buy products in the shop.

Shops need to store information about these cards, such as how many points they contain and who they belong to.

The Boots loyalty card is called the 'Advantage Card'. Boots has over 1400 shops and about 400 of these have an 'Advantage Point'. This is an information point where a customer can insert the card and find out how many points they have to spend. They can also find this out on the Boots website.

The display will show the customer's name, the number of points on the card and how much they are worth

The same details are collected from each Advantage Card holder. This data is stored along with the card number and a points total of zero.

When a customer buys something the points total is updated. Boots keeps a record of the number of points each customer has.

Shops also collect other useful information about customers through their loyalty cards. The computer can record data about what they buy and when and where they buy it. Shops use this data to work out what products are popular, which customers buy what products and much more.

The number of points received and the points total are printed on the till receipt

TALKING POINT 5.2

How do you think shops use the information they collect through loyalty cards? Why is it helpful to them?

Searching for information

Suppose Boots wants to find all cardholders with more than 500 points. Boots has 14 million cardholders so this information can't be found by scrolling down a list. Boots stores all the Advantage Card data in a database. To find information, Boots searches the database. The database allows the computer to search through thousands of records at high speed.

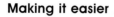

Making it easier

Here is some data that might be stored for five Advantage Card holders:

> James, Byron, 42 Little Road, Nottingham, NE34 8JH, 489, 13, 4/11/04, 7653
> Anna, Svensson, 45 Thornhill, Southampton, SO99 4JD, 48, 2, 29/4/05, 7159
> Emma, Stomp, 17 Portsway, Northampton, NO7 7QT, 79, 14, 12/3/05, 7587
> Alex, Finch, 34 Ashurst Road, Lyndhurst, SO91 6GH, 1345, 4, 25/4/05, 7123
> Chris, Boil, 78 Oak Road, Harlow, CM49 6JD, 426, 6, 28/5/04, 7135

It is not clear what some of this data means. We can put some labels on it to make it clearer.

Field names

Name 1	Name 2	Address	Town	Postcode	Points	Last points	Last used	Branch
James	Byron	42 Little Road	Nottingham	NE34 8JH	489	13	4/11/04	7653
Anna	Svensson	45 Thornhill	Southampton	SO99 4JD	48	2	29/4/05	7159
Emma	Stomp	17 Portsway	Northampton	NO7 7QT	79	14	12/3/05	7587
Alex	Finch	34 Ashurst Road	Lyndhurst	SO91 6GH	1345	4	25/4/05	7123
Chris	Boil	78 Oak Road	Harlow	CM49 6JD	426	6	28/5/04	7135

Record in database

Now the data makes sense. This is what databases are for – storing data in an organised way so you can easily find the information you are looking for.

Every customer has a record with the same data items stored in fields. The column headers are the field names and tell us what each field contains. Now it is easy to sort the records and to search on the different fields.

▶▶Activity 5.2

Look at the data above.

1 How many fields are there? What are the names of the fields? What information do they contain?
2 How many records can you see? Can you explain what a record is?

TALKING POINT 5.3

What fields would you have to search on to find the answers to each question?

> Which cardholders live in London?
>
> Which cardholders live in the Southampton area?
>
> Which cardholders shop in a different area to where they live?
>
> Which customers have more than 2000 points?

When should you use a database?

Databases are useful if you want to store the same set of data for a number of different people, objects or actions.

► **People:** for example, full name, address, phone number, date of birth.

► **Objects:** for example, DVDs in a rental store – title, description, type, rating, etc.

► **Actions:** for example, bookings at a cinema – the customer's name, the date of the performance, the price of the seat etc.

You can then use the database to find things out.

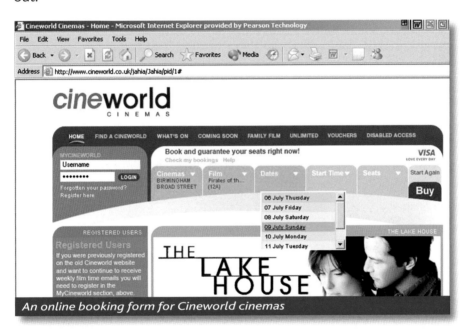

An online booking form for Cineworld cinemas

Cinema	Film	Date	Start time	Total seats
Stockport	The Lake House	05/07/06	20.15	5
Ashford	The Pink Panther	04/07/06	17.45	4
Bishops Stortford	Pirates of the Caribbean	03/07/06	19.30	3
Bedford	RV	03/07/06	19.15	2
Wigan	Curious George	03/07/06	15.10	4
Wigan	Pirates of the Caribbean	04/07/06	19.30	2

This is how the database for the online booking at Cineworld cinemas might look

TALKING POINT 5.4

Think of some situations where a database might be used. Try to think of different examples involving people, objects and actions. Remember – it isn't always obvious that a database is being used.

Many websites are supported by a database. If you can search for information on a website, you are probably using a database without realising it!

▸▸ Activity 5.3

Go to the National Rail website and the Trainline website. Both of these sites use a database to store the train timetable.

1 Search for trains from Chester to London that arrive between 4 and 5 pm next Friday.
2 What differences do you notice between the two websites?
3 What differences do you notice in the way the information is shown?
4 Do you think these websites use the same database?

Hideaways is a holiday cottage letting agency. You can search their website to find a holiday cottage and you can book online. This is possible because the company uses a database to store information about each property.

▸▸ Activity 5.4

1 Look at the Hideaways website.
  ▸ Choose an area of the country that you would like to visit.
  ▸ Choose a week when you want to go on holiday.
    When you click 'Go' a list of properties appears that are available for that week. The database searches for properties that meet your requirements.
2 Name three fields that you think are stored for each cottage.

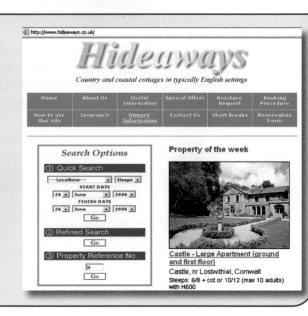

Using a database

Here is an extract from the database used by the Bentley Video Shop.
The video shop rents out and sells DVDs and videos.

Serial No	Title	Rat	Field 4	S/R	Price	Dir	Date
R104	Madagascar	U	Animation	R	£1.99	Eric Darnell/Tom	2005
R125	Harry Potter and the Prisoner of Azkabar	PG	Drama	R	£2.99	Alfonso Cuaron	2004
R117	Clueless	12	Comedy	R	£4.99	Amy Heckerling	1995
S123	Clueless	12	Comedy	S	£8.99	Amy Heckerling	1995
S101	Shrek	U	Animation	S	£11.99	Andrew Adamsor	2001
S104	Finding Nemo	U	Animation	S	£5.99	Andrew Stanton/L	2003
R118	Hitch	12	Comedy	R	£1.99	Andy Tennant	2005
R143	The Island	15	Action	R	£1.99	Anthony Minghell	2005
S125	Romeo and Juliet	12	Drama	S	£12.99	Baz Luhrman	1996
R138	Romeo and Juliet	12	Drama	R	£2.99	Baz Luhrmann	1996
R121	Mission Impossible	PG	Action	R	£3.99	Brian De Palma	1996
S122	Harry Potter and the Chamber of Secrets	PG	Drama	S	£13.99	Chris Columbus	2002

TALKING POINT 5.5

Look at the table above. Is it clear what information is in each field? Can you guess what information each field contains?

The manager at the Bentley Video Shop made improvements to the database. He kept the same information but he changed the field names.

Serial Number	Title	Rating	Category	Sales/rental	Price	Director	Date released
R104	Madagascar	U	Animation	R	£1.99	Eric Darnell/Tom	2005
R125	Harry Potter and the Prisoner of Azkabar	PG	Drama	R	£2.99	Alfonso Cuaron	2004
R117	Clueless	12	Comedy	R	£4.99	Amy Heckerling	1995
S123	Clueless	12	Comedy	S	£8.99	Amy Heckerling	1995
S101	Shrek	U	Animation	S	£11.99	Andrew Adamsor	2001
S104	Finding Nemo	U	Animation	S	£5.99	Andrew Stanton/L	2003
R118	Hitch	12	Comedy	R	£1.99	Andy Tennant	2005
R143	The Island	15	Action	R	£1.99	Anthony Minghell	2005
S125	Romeo and Juliet	12	Drama	S	£12.99	Baz Luhrman	1996
R138	Romeo and Juliet	12	Drama	R	£2.99	Baz Luhrmann	1996
R121	Mission Impossible	PG	Action	R	£3.99	Brian De Palma	1996
R124	Harry Potter and the Chamber of Secrets	PG	Drama	R	£2.99	Chris Columbus	2002

TALKING POINT 5.6

Look at the improved database above. What information does each field contain? Did you guess correctly?

TALKING POINT 5.7

*Open the MEALS database for **THE PROJECT**. What is the purpose of the database? What are the field names? What information is stored in each field?*

Entering, editing and deleting information

You have now looked at some databases and have discovered how they store information. In the SPB you will need to be able to enter, edit and delete data records from a database.

You can enter new database records by typing straight into the table. However, other people might not understand your field names or might not be familiar with the software. A data entry form solves this problem. A data entry form makes it clear to the user what information needs to be entered. The fields can also be labelled in a user-friendly way.

Creating a data entry form

The person filling in a data entry form might not know much about what is in the database. Therefore, it should be very clear what information they need to enter in each field.

TALKING POINT 5.8

Look at the data entry form for the FILMS database. It is not very user friendly. What would you do to improve it?

Serial No	R104
Title	Madagascar
Rat	U
Field 4	Animation
S/R	R
Price	£1.99
Dir	Eric Darnell/Tom McGrath
Date	2005

Wizards are not magic!

You can use a wizard to help you create a data entry form. However, you will need to customise the form yourself to make it fit for purpose.

Customising a data entry form

Heading

Your heading should clearly tell the user what the form is for. Don't let a wizard do it for you without checking that it makes sense.

Labels

Each data entry field needs a label to tell the user what it is. The wizard will try to use the field names from the database. These do not always make sense. Make sure the labels will make sense to everyone.

Layout

A good layout will make your form easier to use. The fields should be grouped together in a sensible way, for example the different lines of an address. It should also be clear which labels go with which fields. Make sure there is plenty of white space so the form is not cluttered. If your form is too cramped, it will be difficult to read.

Fonts

Use fonts that are easy to read on screen. Arial and Verdana are good. You might want to use different fonts for field labels and for the data to be entered. Make sure the title stands out.

TALKING POINT 5.9

Look at the adapted data entry form for the FILMS database. What changes have been made to the version in Talking Point 5.8? Are these changes helpful? What else would you do to improve it?

Bentley's Vi	
Serial Number	R100
Film Title	Serenity
Rating	15
Category	Action
Sale or Rental	R
Price	£2.99
Director	Joss Whedon
Date released	2005

▶▶**Activity 5.5**

Open the FILMS database and save it in your user area.
Make the following changes.

1 Using the data entry form, enter a new record for *Mission Impossible II*.

2 Delete the records for *Grease 2 and Home Alone 3*.

3 Change the price of *Notting Hill* and *Shrek* to £8.99.

4 Change the rating for *The Lion King* to U.

TALKING POINT 5.10

Did you find the data entry form easy to use? How could it be improved?

A clear layout is very important. It might help to sketch out a layout on paper before you make changes on the data entry form.

▶▶**Activity 5.6**

The layout on the FILMS data entry form is still poor.

1 On paper, design a layout that would be more user friendly. Think about how you will group the fields and remember to use plenty of white space.

2 Using your design, change the layout of the form.

▶▶**Activity 5.7**

1 You are going to design a data entry form for the MEALS database in THE PROJECT. Look at the database and ask yourself:

▶ What heading will you give the form?

▶ What information does each field contain?

▶ How will you label each of the fields?

2 Decide how you will group the fields together and design a draft layout on paper.

Choose effective colours

Make sure there is a good contrast between the text and the background.

Help messages

You can also provide help messages to help the user. These can be entered in text boxes on the form. For example, for the 'Sales or Rental' field in the FILMS database you could add the message:

> Enter S (Sales)
>
> R (Rental)

TALKING POINT 5.11

What help message could you add for the 'Rating' field in the data entry form for the FILMS database?

▶▶ Activity 5.8

Look at the design you started in Activity 5.7.

1 **Decide where help messages would be useful.**
2 **Add help messages to your design.**
3 **Show your design to others in your group and get feedback. Make improvements.**

Can I do this?

Using database tools, make sure that you can:

Create a data entry form

Select fields for the form

Enter a suitable title

Enter labels

Change colours and formatting

▶▶ Activity 5.9

1 **Use a wizard to create a data entry form for the MEALS database.**
2 **Compare the form with your design. What changes do you need to make?**
3 **Change the form so it matches your design.**
4 **Show the form to two other students and get feedback using this form from THE PROJECT brief. Make changes.**

Getting the data right

When you store information in a database you must make sure that the data you put in is accurate.

TALKING POINT 5.12

Why is it important to enter data correctly into a database? Why would it be bad for business if data was entered incorrectly in the FILMS database?

What is validation?

Validation means checking data as it is entered to prevent errors. Validation rules can be set up to make sure the right kind of data is entered into each field. For example, a field asking for 'Name' can be set up so it will not accept a number. A field asking for 'Age' can be set up not to accept text. Alternatively, rules can be set up so that a field will only accept certain inputs, e.g. U, PG, 15, 18 for 'Rating' in the FILMS database. Or a field can be set up to accept numbers within a certain range, for example under £30 for 'Price' in the FILMS database.

TALKING POINT 5.13

Why is validation important? Can you think of some examples of when it might be used?

Validation messages

When invalid data is added, you get a validation message. If you don't create your own validation message, the software will probably display a default message.

It is possible to change validation messages so they are more user friendly.

▸▸ Activity 5.10

Enter the following information into the FILMS database and see what happens:

▶ *111.99* **under 'Sales price' in the record for** *Toy Story*
▶ *10* **under 'Rating' in the record for** *Charlie's Angels*
▶ *For sale* **under 'Sales/Rental' in the record for** *Armageddon*.

Why are these messages there? Are they helpful?

TALKING POINT 5.14

Look at these examples of validation messages. Some of them are the default messages and some have been made more user friendly. Can you tell which ones? What does each message mean? Which messages mean the same thing? Which are most useful?

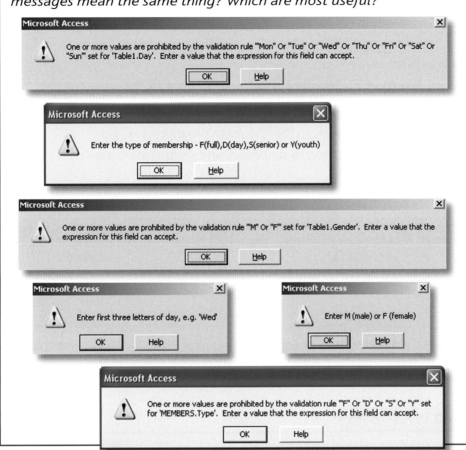

Can I do this?

Using database tools, make sure you can:

Edit validation messages

▶▶Activity 5.11

Enter the information in the document 'New Record' into MEALS database for THE PROJECT. What message did you get when you entered '*pudding*' into the 'Type' fields. What does it mean?

1 **In pairs, discuss how you would make this message more user friendly.**
2 **Try out your ideas on another pair. Get feedback and make improvements if necessary.**
3 **Open the database and make changes to the validation message.**

Extracting information

Databases are all about finding things out. You can search databases for specific information quickly and easily.

Searching on one field

Sometimes your search will be simple. For example, if you want to search the FILMS database for all films that cost £11.99 exactly you can enter the criterion **11.99** in the Sales cost field. However, if you want to search for all films costing less than £11.99 you cannot use the criterion **less than 11.99**. The correct criterion is **<11.99**.

If you want to search a database, you must tell it what you want using the correct language. The database program does not understand instructions written in sentences and so operators are used as a form of shorthand.

Here are some examples:

Operator	What the symbols mean	Example	Means
<	Less than	<10	Less than 10
<=	Less than or equal to	<=10	Less than 10 or exactly equal to 10
>	Greater than	>50	Greater than 50
>=	Greater than or equal to	>=50	Greater than 50 or exactly equal to 50

TALKING POINT 5.15

What do the following criteria mean?
>30   <=21   >=9.99   <21

You must make sure you use the correct operator when you search a database. It can cause a lot of problems if you get it wrong.

TALKING POINT 5.16

The bar manager at Bentley Sports and Social club wanted a list of all members aged 18 or over who can drink alcohol. He entered the search criterion <=18 into the club's members database. What went wrong? What criterion should he have entered?

Searching with text

If you are entering text, check that it matches the text in the table. For example, if you are searching for 'February' and there are no results, it may be because the months are stored as Jan, Feb, Mar, etc.

Checking search results

Just because you get some search results, it doesn't mean they are correct. Always check your results for errors.

Title	Price
▶ Pride and Prejudice	£15.99
Harry Potter and the Chamber of Secrets	£13.99
Romeo and Juliet	£12.99
*	£0.00

When looking at the results, remind yourself of what you were trying to find out. Have you found what you need?

Look at these search results. The search was supposed to find all films that cost £11.99 or more. However, it doesn't show any films that cost £11.99 *exactly*. This is because **>11.99** was used as the search criterion. It should have been **>=11.99**

Choosing the fields you need

You don't always need to see all fields when you run a search. For example, you might want to know the titles of all films with a PG rating, but not who directed them.

When you search, you can choose which fields to include in the results. Make sure you include all the fields you need. If in doubt, leave a field in. You can always take it out later.

▸▸ Activity 5.12

Imagine you are going to produce the following publications:

- ▶ a leaflet listing films by popular directors
- ▶ a list of films available to rent
- ▶ a poster advertising action films.

What information will you need from the database? Which fields will you include in your search results?

Why save searches?

You might want to use searches more than once. It makes sense to save searches just in case. Make sure that you give your searches sensible names. Don't save searches as 'Search 1' or 'Query 1' – you will never remember what they contain.

TALKING POINT 5.17

Discuss different file names for the searches in Activity 5.12.

5

Can I do this?

Using database software, make sure that you can:

Search on a single field

Select fields to include in results

Use relational operators

Sort on one field

Use logical operators

Search on more than one field

The manager of the Bentley Video Shop wants to advertise his shop in the local toy library. He needs to know how many films he has which are suitable for children under four years of age.

TALKING POINT 5.18

What field do you need to search in to find films suitable for children under four? What criteria will you enter? What fields will you include in your search results?

▶▶Activity 5.13

Carry out the search and save it using a sensible name. Don't forget to check your results.

Compare your results with a partner and discuss any differences.

The manager also wants to promote his low priced videos and DVDs. He wants to put a poster in the shop window showing which films are available to buy for £8.99 or less.

▶▶Activity 5.14

What operator will you need to search for films costing £8.99 or less? Carry out the search and save it using a sensible name. Check your results.

Sorting a database table

You can sort data in a database table in different ways. This makes it easier to find information.

You will be asked to sort in ascending or descending order. Ascending means starting with the lowest and moving upwards (e.g. 1, 2, 3, 4, 5 or A, B, C, D). Descending means starting with the highest and moving down (e.g. 5, 4, 3, 2, 1 or D, C, B, A).

Title	Price
Mary Poppins	£4.99
Finding Nemo	£5.99
The Terminal	£5.99
The Lion King	£7.99
Goodbye Lenin	£7.99
Bend It Like Beckha	£7.99
Star Wars Episode I	£8.99
Toy Story II	£8.99
Goal!	£8.99
Harry Potter and The	£8.99
Clueless	£8.99
A Cinderella Story	£9.99
Batman Returns	£9.99
Star Wars Episode I	£9.99

These films are sorted by price in ascending order

▸▸Activity 5.15

Look again at the MEALS database for THE PROJECT. You have been asked what options there are for vegetarians and how much they cost.

1 How would you find this information using a search? Why might it be useful to sort the results? How would you sort them?
2 Carry out your search and check your results.
3 Carry out your sort.

AND and OR

You have already looked at using operators to search on one criterion. This means searching for just one thing, for example all films that cost more than £3.99. If you want to search for more than one thing in the same field you must use the operators AND and OR.

▶ OR finds records containing either one criterion or another. For example:

PG OR U in the rating field will find all films that are either PG or U certificate.

Comedy OR Drama in the type field will find all comedy and all drama films.

▶ AND finds records where both criteria are true. For example, between two values.

>=9 AND <=12 in the sales price field would find all the DVDs that cost £9 or over *and* less than £12.

TALKING POINT 5.19

What results would you find if you entered the following criteria when searching the MEALS database?

▶ *>100 AND <250* in the 'Calories' field
▶ *>=100 AND <=250* in the 'Calories' field
▶ *100 OR 250* in the 'Calories' field

▸▸Activity 5.16

What fields would you search and which criteria would you use to find the following in the FILMS database:

▶ films with a rental price between £2.99 and £3.99
▶ films directed by Steven Spielberg or James Cameron
▶ animation and comedy films.

Carry out these searches and compare results. Discuss any differences.

Searching on more than one field

Sometimes you will need to search on more than one field. If you wanted to find films directed by Steven Spielberg with a PG rating you would search on the 'Director' and 'Rating' fields.

Put one search criterion in at a time and check your results before you search on the next field. Don't assume the search is correct just because some records are found.

▶▶Activity 5.17

You are going to search for films which have a U rating and are also animation films.

1 **What fields will you search on?**
2 **What operators, if any, will you need in each field?**
3 **Search on the first field. Check your results.**
4 **Search on the second field. Check your results. Compare your results with a partner and discuss any differences.**
5 **Now repeat 1-4 for the following searches:**
   ▶ **films priced £11.99 with a PG or 15 rating**
   ▶ **comedy and drama films with a PG rating.**

Database reports

The main purpose of a database is to provide information. It is essential that the information makes sense to your audience. Database reports help you present that information in an effective way.

There is more on database reports on pages 124–5. This deals with how to present database reports effectively.

Action films

Film	Rating	Category	Sales/rental	Price
Batman	PG	Action	Rental	£1.99
Batman Begins	12	Action	Rental	£4.99
Batman Returns	PG	Action	Sales	£9.99
Batman Returns	PG	Action	Rental	£3.99
Charlie's Angels	15	Action	Rental	£2.99
Jurasic Park III	PG	Action	Rental	£3.99
Jurasic Park III	PG	Action	Sales	£10.99
King Kong	12	Action	Rental	£2.99
Mission Impossible	PG	Action	Rental	£3.99
Mission Impossible II	15	Action	Rental	£2.99
Pirates of the Caribbean	12	Action	Sales	£11.99
Pirates of the Caribbean	12	Action	Rental	£2.99
Serenity	15	Action	Rental	£2.99
The Island	15	Action	Rental	£1.99

A database report showing action films

Other uses of database information

You can use information from databases in lots of different publications.

Copying and pasting

You can copy and paste sections of your database table into other publications. For example, if you were doing a presentation on low-fat vegetarian foods, you could search your database then copy your results table into a presentation slide.

Different formats

Sometimes a database table will not be the most effective format. If you wanted to make a poster advertising low-price cartoon films, you would not include a database table. That would not be very eye-catching! You could search your database for the relevant information then put it into a more attractive format.

Different purposes

The Boots Advantage Card database holds information about what products each customer buys. Suppose Boots wanted to send out details of an offer on baby food to customers. They would want to send the information only to people who have children. They could search the database for the customers who often buy baby food or nappies to find these people.

Remember audience and purpose!

However you use information from your database, make sure it is presented in a way that is fit for audience and purpose.

TALKING POINT 5.20

How would you use information from the MEALS database in THE PROJECT in the following publications? Think about what information you would need and how you would present it.

▶ *A poster advertising low-price diabetic foods*

▶ *A leaflet on low-fat foods*

▶ *A report to students on vegetarian, low-calorie foods.*

Tackling **THE PROJECT**

P

Data entry

Look at the section on 'Using a database' in **THE PROJECT** brief. You have already:

▶ looked at the MEALS database (see Talking Point 5.7)

▶ created a data entry form to add new records and got feedback on it (see Activities 5.8 and 5.9)

You will learn how to save evidence of your data entry form in Chapter 9.

Adding information

Look at the 'Using a database' section in **THE PROJECT** brief. Using your data entry form, add the records saved in the file 'newmeals'.

Searches

Now look at the 'Database reports' section of the website. You have already designed one search (see Activity 5.15). Now design the other searches that you need. Think about whether you want to include this information in any of your publications. If you do, don't forget to update your SOURCES and PLAN FOR GATHERING INFO documents.

You will learn how to save evidence of your search designs in Chapter 9.

Reports

You will learn how to produce database reports in Chapter 8.

6 Getting the message across – attracting attention

How do you get a message across to busy people on the move? You need to attract their attention and get your message across in seconds. Posters are a great way of doing this.

If you want to send information to people directly, you can use a flyer. Flyers are smaller than posters, but can contain more information. People can take more time to read them as they are given their own copy.

A good poster or flyer takes time to design and produce. Space is limited, so you must think carefully about what to include and where to put it. You won't have room for extras so everything must have a purpose.

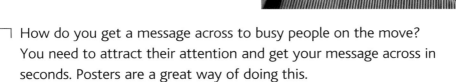

In this chapter you will learn how to attract attention by:

▶ *designing posters and flyers for specific audiences and purposes*
▶ *selecting appropriate images and text*
▶ *combining components to get the message across*
▶ *prototyping, testing and improving your designs*

Posters

What do posters aim to do?

Stop them in their tracks!

You cannot be sure who will see a poster or who will read it. You can try to target a particular audience by choosing where to display it, but it must be eye-catching so people will stop to look.

Let your poster do the talking!

You will not be around when people read your poster so they will not be able to ask questions if it doesn't make sense. It must give a clear message.

Cleaner farms
Better flocks

Keeping out disease and harmful bacteria

www.food.gov.uk

FOOD STANDARDS AGENCY

> **TALKING POINT 6.1**
>
> *Look at this poster. What is its purpose? What message does it try to communicate? Who is it aimed at? Are they likely to stop and read it?*

Don't waffle!

The amount you can say is limited by the size of the poster – it's not like a leaflet or a website where you can have as many pages as you like. Use as few words as possible and keep the language simple.

> **TALKING POINT 6.2**
>
> *Look at this poster. How could it be improved?*
>
> *Ask yourself:*
> - *Is the text suitable for a poster?*
> - *Is there enough detail or too much?*
> - *Are the messages clear?*
> - *Is the design effective?*

Get the size right

If you print a poster yourself, you will be limited by the size of paper your printer can cope with. Printing firms will print any size of poster, but this can be expensive.

You also need to think about the amount of space you have to display the poster. Local shops will often put posters up, but they have limited space and may prefer smaller posters.

Flyers

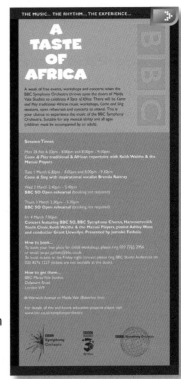

TALKING POINT 6.3

What is the difference between a flyer and a poster?

Who are flyers for?

▶ Flyers are intended for individual people.

▶ Sometimes they are delivered to specific people, for instance, via the post.

▶ Flyers allow people to have their own copy of the information.

What makes a good flyer?

▶ An appropriate size. A5 is popular because it fits through letterboxes.

▶ Good use of space.

▶ An eye-catching design.

▶ Text and images that are high quality and easy to read.

TALKING POINT 6.4

Look at the two examples of flyers on this page. Which features do you think work well? Are there any features you don't like?

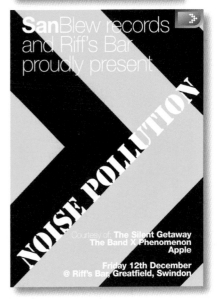

▶▶ Activity 6.1

Work as a group to collect examples of flyers and posters. Choose some examples that are effective and some that are not. Try to identify the audience and purpose for each.

TALKING POINT 6.5

Show the examples you have collected. Discuss which examples work well and which don't and give reasons.
Ask yourself:

▶ *Where might it be displayed?*
▶ *Is the text easy to understand? Is there enough or too much? Is the message clear?*
▶ *Are the images eye-catching? Do they help get the message across?*
▶ *Is the design effective? Is the layout clear or confusing? Is the flyer/poster easy to read?*

Discuss how you might improve each flyer and poster.

Bentley Charity Ball

To help us through the rest of this chapter we will use a scenario. This gives us a purpose and a target audience for what we are doing.

Scenario

Bentley Town Council is planning a charity ball in aid of Children in Need.

The event organiser needs a poster and flyer to advertise the ball.

Open this file and read the full details.

TALKING POINT 6.6

Who *is the audience for the flyer and poster?*
Why *are the flyer and poster needed?*
Where *will the publications be displayed or read?*

▶▶Activity 6.2

What should the poster for Bentley Charity Ball include?
Produce some notes or a mind map. Ask yourself:

▶ **Who is the audience and what is the purpose?**
▶ **How will the poster attract the target audience?**
▶ **How much information do you need to include?**

▶▶Activity 6.3

What should the flyer for Bentley Charity Ball include?
Produce some notes or a mind map. Ask yourself:

▶ **Who is the audience and what is the purpose?**
▶ **How will the flyer attract the target audience?**
▶ **What style of language is appropriate?**

Designing posters and flyers

There is nothing worse than a badly designed poster! It might even put people off completely.

Choosing colours

- ▶ **How many?** Don't use too many colours – it can look messy.

- ▶ **What shades?** Light pastel shades give a very different effect to bright or dark colours.

- ▶ **Contrast?** Choose background and foreground colours that work well together. The foreground and text should stand out.

- ▶ **Headings** can be highlighted by using different colour combinations to the rest of the page.

TALKING POINT 6.7

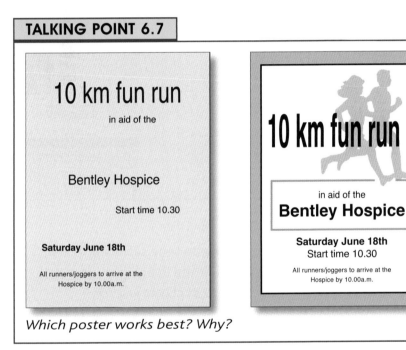

Which poster works best? Why?

Choosing fonts

- ▶ **How many?** As few as possible! Too many font types look messy.

- ▶ **Which styles?** Choose fonts that are easy to read.

- ▶ **What sizes?** Choose the size according to the importance of the text.

- ▶ **What case?** Do not use all UPPER CASE type in your posters. It can make the text difficult to read.

THIS IS WHAT IT LOOKS LIKE WHEN ALL THE CHARACTERS ARE IN UPPER CASE

This is what it looks like when only the first character is in upper case

Death by word art!

Use word art only if it improves your design.
It must serve a purpose. If in doubt, leave it out!

A picture is worth a thousand words

Photographs and other images can be very effective if you make sure that they are:

▶ appropriate

▶ positioned correctly

▶ good quality

▶ not distorted.

Remember that you must have permission to use images if they belong to someone else

---

TALKING POINT 6.8

Look at this design for the opening page of Chapter 6. What is wrong with it? Compare it with page 85 in this book.

Getting the message across – attracting attention

⋗ Digimodule

How do you get a message across to busy people on the move? They don't have time to stop and read lots of information. You need to attract their attention and get your message across to them in seconds. You've guessed it, you need a poster!

Posters can be used to announce an event such as a disco or a sale, promote a service or new product or to campaign for something.

However good your poster, the audience will be limited to those who see it. What if you want to get the information to more people? This is where flyers come in. They can be delivered through doors or left in public places. Although flyers are smaller, they can contain more information. Each person gets their own copy so they can take their time to read the content.

A good poster or flyer takes time to design and produce. Space is limited, so what you choose to include and where you put it is very important. Everything must have a purpose.

In this chapter you will learn how to attract attention by:
▶ designing posters and flyers for specific audiences and purposes
▶ selecting appropriate images and text
▶ combining components to produce effective posters and flyers
▶ using prototyping and feedback to ensure that you get the message across

---

Death by clipart!

Choosing clipart can be fun, but you can easily waste time searching through clipart images. Always have a clear idea of the image you are looking for before you start. Never include a piece of clipart just for the sake of it.

Borders

Page borders sometimes look effective. However, if there is already a lot of information on a page, the border can make it look crowded.

Borders and lines can also be used within a page to make a particular section stand out.

Layout

Once you have decided on all the items that must appear on your poster, you can concentrate on the layout.

▶ Make the most of the space, but don't try to squash in too much.

▶ Don't put things in random places. Think carefully about which items should be grouped together.

White space

White space is any empty space on a page.

Don't be afraid to have plenty of white space on a poster. It helps the reader see each part clearly.

White space is also important on a flyer. Use it to separate different parts of your flyer. This helps the reader take in one section at a time.

Alignment

Try right and left alignment as well as centring each block of text to see what looks best.

> **Can I do this?**
>
> Using word processing or desktop publishing tools, make sure you can:
>
> **Format text**
> **Align text**
> **Change colours**
> **Use lines and borders**

TALKING POINT 6.9

How could this menu be improved?

▸▸Activity 6.4

Look at this poster. The various items have been scattered about in a random way.

Organise the items into an effective layout. Change the font style and size if necessary.

▸▸Activity 6.5

1 On paper, produce designs for a poster and a flyer for the Bentley Charity Ball. Use the scenario and the notes you made for Activities 6.2 and 6.3.
2 Show your designs to other people and ask them to give you feedback.
3 Make improvements as a result of the feedback.

6

Creating posters and flyers

Word processing tools have many features that can help you to produce an excellent poster. You can also use desktop publishing tools.

Can I do this?

Using word processing or desktop publishing tools, make sure you can:

Use text boxes

Wrap text

Import and position images

Crop and resize images

Use spelling and grammar checkers

Proofread for other errors

▸ Activity 6.6

Use your designs from Activity 6.5 to produce a poster and a flyer for the Bentley Charity Ball.

Keep an eye on file sizes. If your files take up megabytes (MB) they will be using a lot of space.

Review, review and review

Keep checking your work as you go along. Produce draft versions or prototypes and check them.

Here is a checklist to use when testing prototypes. You can use it when reviewing your own work, or give it to someone who is going to look at your work and give you feedback.

Ask others to give feedback on your work

Proofreading

Proofreading means checking for spelling or grammar mistakes.

The spellchecker is useful, but it is *not* always right! Don't rely on it to find all your spelling mistakes, and don't trust it to suggest the right word. Sometimes you might type in the wrong word and the spellchecker won't pick this up.

Always ask someone to check your spellings. Even professional writers do this.

▶ Activity 6.7

Type each pair of sentences into a word processing document and run a spell check. Does the spellchecker always help you?

Sentence One	Sentence Two	Which is the correct sentence? Did the spell checker tell you?
They said there team would win.	They said their team would win.	
The student could not here the lecturer.	The student could not hear the lecturer.	
I use my PC all the time.	I use my pea sea all the time.	
I love to write stories.	I love to right stories.	
I don't like reading bucks.	I don't like reading books.	
My mum will give me a cheque for the school trip.	My mum will give me a check for the school trip.	
When should we meet up to discuss THE PROJECT?	When should we meat up to discuss THE PROJECT?	

Test users and feedback

It is important to find out what other people think of your publications. Find some people who are part of your target audience for the publication, or who have similar interests. Ask them to comment on your publication. For instance, if a poster is aimed at young children, ask young children for feedback. If a flyer is aimed at parents, ask parents what they think.

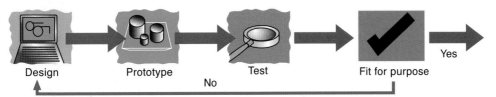

Remember to follow the production cycle. Keep going back to the design stage until the publication is fit for purpose.

▶ Activity 6.8

1 Ask your classmates to give you feedback on your poster and flyer for the Bentley Charity Ball. Ask them to use the checklist.
2 Keep a record of the feedback you receive and the changes you make.
3 Once you have made the changes, test your publications again and proofread them.

Tackling **The Project**

Now it is time to complete your poster and flyer for **The Project**. They need to attract attention and interest people in the target audience.

Re-read the 'Flyer' and 'Poster' sections of **The Project** brief. Now look at the plans for the poster and flyer that you produced in Chapters 2 and 3. Are you still happy with them?

For each publication, make sure you have all the information you need.

Start by designing the layout. Remember the lessons you learnt when you were producing the Bentley Charity Ball publications. You should have all the images and text that you need, but it is not too late to add more or change them.

Create your publication. Don't forget to proofread it carefully.

Ask for feedback from suitable test users. Make any necessary changes. Review your final publications.

Save your final versions, prototypes and feedback. You will find out about how to produce acceptable file formats in Chapter 9.

7 Getting the message across – making information available

In Chapter 6 we looked at how to attract attention – how to give people information that they didn't know they were looking for.

This chapter has a different focus. It's all about providing publications for people who are actively looking for information. The information is often very important to them. They want reliable, clear information that is attractive and easy to use. They want the information to be available in a way that suits them.

Leaflets, information points and web pages can all do the job, but only if they are well designed. Are you ready for the challenge?

In this chapter you will learn how to make information available by:

► *identifying the type of audience and where they might look*
► *designing web pages, information points and leaflets*
► *combining components to produce effective publications*
► *using prototyping and feedback to ensure that you get your message across*

Websites

Websites have a number of advantages:

▶ it is possible to reach people all over the world

▶ it is easy to keep the information up to date

▶ the audience can be of unlimited size at no extra cost

▶ there is no limit to the amount of information you can include

▶ users can access the information 24 hours a day, seven days a week.

TALKING POINT 7.1

Look at this website.

What is its purpose?

Who is it aimed at?

What message does it communicate?

How easy is it to use this site?

Do you think young people will be attracted to the site?

What makes an effective website?

It must be easy for visitors to find their way around a website. The information should be clearly organised to let people know where to look for the information they want. Websites can easily become overloaded with information as there is no limit to the number of pages. Planning is essential to the success of any website.

▶▶ Activity 7.1

Explore the BBC website. Comment on some of the features of the site. Use this worksheet to help you.

Designing web pages

Text

Avoid long passages of text. Users don't like too much scrolling. Keep the text simple and to the point.

Fonts

Use as few font styles as possible. Use font sizes to show what is important ... and what is less important.

Choose fonts that are easy to read. Verdana and Georgia are good as they were designed specifically for web pages.

Layout

Keep the layout simple. Align the blocks of text so that they look neat and tidy.

Use headings and sub-headings to help the user find what they are looking for.

Bullets can be used for lists. Make sure that bullets are consistent in style, size and line spacing.

Avoid narrow columns. They can make text hard to follow.

What is wrong with this design?

▶▶ Activity 7.2

1 **Open this file using the software you use for producing web pages.**
2 **Format the text to make it easier to read.**
3 **Lay out the page neatly.**
4 **Preview the page in your browser and ask others for feedback.**
5 **Save your file as OASISSWIM.**

Oasis Swimming
Classes
Run by our qualified instructors. Application forms from reception.
Early birds aqua aerobics
6:30-7 a.m. Monday, Wednesday and Friday
This session will get you off to a flying start
Aqua tots
2-3 p.m. Tuesday, Saturday
Help your child grow in confidence in the water.
Aqua fit
10-11 a.m. Tuesday and Thursday
You don't need to be able to swim to enjoy this session of gentle exercises. Designed for those who want to avoid anything too strenuous
High jumps
7-8 p.m. Thursday
Introductory diving course. Over 14s only.
Swimming lessons
7-8 p.m.
Beginners: Monday
Intermediate: Wednesday
Special sessions
Just turn up
Adults only swim
8-9 p.m. Monday-Friday
This session is free from hustle and bustle. Soothing music to help you relax and re-energise.
Chart swim
7-8 p.m. Tuesday
Swim along to the latest chart hits
Private pool hire
Hire the pool for private functions
Clubs
Several clubs are based at the pool. Details of their sessions are available from reception

Using images

An image could be a photograph, a cartoon, a map or a drawing. Images make a page more lively. They can also give information in their own right.

Gathering images

Only include images that help to get the message across. Never include an image just for the sake of it. Use ready-made images if they are suitable, but remember that you must have permission to use them if they belong to someone else.

You could also create your own image. See Chapter 3 for information about capturing and creating images.

Deciding where to put images

If an image goes with a piece of text, make sure you position it so that it is obvious which text it goes with. Allow some white space around each image.

Make sure images are not distorted

When making an image bigger or smaller, be careful to keep the same proportions. Always drag a corner handle so that the image does not get squeezed or stretched.

Which one of these images has the correct proportions?

Resolution

Resolution is a measure of the quality of an image: the higher the resolution, the better the quality. Images on screen can be at a lower resolution than for print. However, you must use browser tools to preview images and make sure that they look good enough.

Think carefully when using images on web pages: the higher the resolution the bigger the file size will be. If the file size is big, the image will take more time to download, which can be irritating for the user.

Remember that resizing an image once you have inserted it into a web page does not alter its file size.

Selecting the file format

Images can be stored in several different file formats. For instance:

▶ GIF (.gif) for drawings with blocks of colour

▶ JPEG (.jpg) for photos.

When you do your SPB you will be told which file formats you can use.

This high resolution image is suitable for print but might not be good for a website

TALKING POINT 7.2

What will happen if you include lots of high resolution images in a website? Why is this a problem? What can you do instead?

Accessibility

Not everyone will be able to view the images on a web page. People who are visually impaired use special software that reads just the text. Every image should have a text description of what the image shows. This is called alternative text.

Adding sound

You can use sound to make a web page more interesting. For example, music can create a particular mood. A voice recording can provide additional information.

However, not all computer systems have sound. Don't rely on sound for essential information.

Make sure that any sound files you use for the SPB are in the list of acceptable formats.

Now I know what it was like to watch silent movies.

Choosing colours

▶ **Which colours?**

Web-safe colours will display correctly on any computer. If you are using web authoring software, you can select the Web-Safe Palette.

▶ **How many?**

Don't use too many colours — it can make your web page look messy and confusing.

▶ **What shades?**

Light pastel shades give a very different effect from bright or dark colours.

▶ **Contrast?**

- Use dark text on light backgrounds.
- Use light text on dark backgrounds.
- Don't put red text on green (or green on red). Some people cannot tell red and green apart.

DiDA Designed to develop real-world practical skills	DiDA Designed to develop real-world practical skills	DiDA Designed to develop real-world practical skills	**DiDA** Designed to develop real-world practical skills
DiDA Designed to develop real-world	**DiDA** Designed to develop real-world		**DiDA** Designed to develop real-world practical skills

Some good and bad colour combinations.

▶▶ Activity 7.3

Using web tools, open the file OASISSWIM you created for Activity 7.2. Experiment with different combinations of web-safe colours. Which combinations are the most effective and easy to read?

Using links

Although you do not need to develop a complete website, you need to add links to your web pages so that users can move around easily.

You are likely to use two types of link:

▶ **Internal link.** This goes to another page on the same website. There must be at least one of these on every page so that the user can move on easily.

▶ **External link.** This goes to a different website.

Plan your links carefully. You could do this by sketching a diagram of how the pages link together on paper.

Entering a path

Whenever you create a link to another page or website, you need to enter its path or address. You can learn more about this on pages 150 and 151.

Identifying links

You need to make links obvious to the user. Text links use words as links. These words or phrases are underlined or in a different colour to show that they are links. The user clicks the text to move to a new page or site.

An image link can be an image or a button that the user must click.

▶▶ Activity 7.4

Look at the websites for the BBC, Amazon and ASOS. Find examples of:

▶ text links
▶ image links
▶ internal links
▶ external links.

Also look for links that take you back to the top of long pages.

Storyboarding

Storyboards are used to plan websites. They help you to plan:

- how many pages you need
- what components will appear on every page
- the position of components on each page
- the links between pages
- colours and styles.

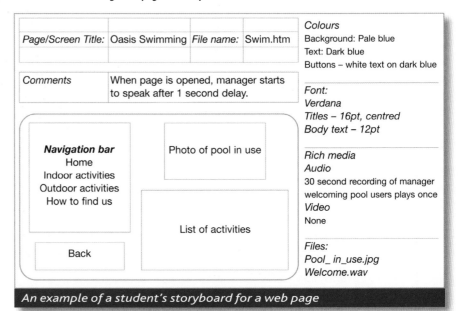

Page/Screen Title:	Oasis Swimming	File name:	Swim.htm

Comments: When page is opened, manager starts to speak after 1 second delay.

Navigation bar
Home
Indoor activities
Outdoor activities
How to find us

Back

Photo of pool in use

List of activities

Colours
Background: Pale blue
Text: Dark blue
Buttons – white text on dark blue

Font:
Verdana
Titles – 16pt, centred
Body text – 12pt

Rich media
Audio
30 second recording of manager welcoming pool users plays once
Video
None

Files:
Pool_ in_use.jpg
Welcome.wav

An example of a student's storyboard for a web page

A storyboard can be done on paper or on screen. Many designers like to start on paper and then create an electronic version. Either way, make sure you include enough detail to show others what you plan to do.

Consistency

Each page of a website contains different information, but all the pages should have the same look, feel and style.

▶▶ Activity 7.5

Look at these web pages. They all belong to the same site, but they look and feel different.

1 How would you change them to make them more consistent?
2 How else could you improve them?

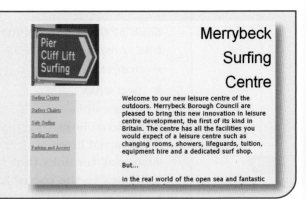

Pier
Cliff Lift
Surfing

Surfing Centre
Surfers Chalets
Safe Surfing
Surfing Zones
Parking and Access

Merrybeck
Surfing
Centre

Welcome to our new leisure centre of the outdoors. Merrybeck Borough Council are pleased to bring this new innovation in leisure centre development, the first of its kind in Britain. The centre has all the facilities you would expect of a leisure centre such as changing rooms, showers, lifeguards, tuition, equipment hire and a dedicated surf shop.

But...

In the real world of the open sea and fantastic

▶▶ Activity 7.6

1 Re-read the scenario for the Bentley Charity Ball.
2 Design a storyboard for four web pages about the ball. These will be published on the council website with a link from the home page. Make sure your pages are consistent.
3 Ask other people to give you feedback. Make changes based on this feedback.

Designing an information point

An information point provides screen-based information in one place. It is not uploaded onto the web; it just runs on an individual computer. The ones shown here run on specially designed machines, but any PC can be set up as an information point.

An information point offers information to people who visit a particular place. They might be shoppers at a shopping centre, rail travellers at a station or visitors at a theme park. If you want to design an information point, you will have some idea of who the audience is likely to be.

A fully interactive information point can be created using web authoring software. However, you might prefer to use other tools, such as presentation software.

Persuade people to use it

Imagine people are milling around at a theme park. They will see the information point, but they might not use it. It will need to attract their attention and be very useful.

Make it easy to use

People using an information point may not be familiar with computers. It has to be easy to use so that people can find the information they need.

▸▸Activity 7.7

In Chapter 3 you did some work towards the information point on healthy eating. Now you are going to use a storyboard to design the information point.

1 Produce a storyboard for your home page. The home page should clearly show what information is available on the information point. It should have links to each area of the information point.
2 Now produce a storyboard for the other pages of the information point.
3 Save your storyboards in the correct folder.

Creating web pages and information points

Choosing your tools

What are the options for web pages?

For Unit 1, you have to create and link a few web pages. You do not have to produce a whole website. You can use specialist web authoring software such as Dreamweaver or FrontPage, or you can use the web tools of word processing or desktop publishing software.

Can I do this?

Using web authoring tools, make sure that you can:

Format text	**Use a table for page layout**
Use bullets	**Align text**
Change colours	**Use lines and borders**
Import and position images	**Align text and images**
Crop and resize images	**Optimise images**
Insert links	**Use text and images as links**

▶▶Activity 7.8

Use your storyboard from Activity 7.6 to produce some web pages for the Bentley Charity Ball.

What are the options for information points?

You can create an information point using the same tools that you use for your web pages. Presentation software can also work. You will have a chance to try this out on the **Tackling THE PROJECT** pages. If you choose presentation software, these are the skills you will need.

Can I do this?

Using presentation software, make sure you can:

Create slides	**Create and use a master slide**
Use lines and borders	**Change colours**
Import and position images	**Align text and images**
Crop and resize images	**Include animation**
Include sound	**Insert links**
Create transitions	

> ## ▶▶Activity 7.9
>
> **Look again at the storyboard you produced for Activity 7.6.
> Using presentation software, create the home page for your
> information point.**

Keep on checking!

Check prototype versions of your pages by asking the following
questions:

- ▶ Are there any spelling or grammar mistakes?
- ▶ Is the text easy to understand?
- ▶ Is the style suitable and consistent?
- ▶ Is the layout clear?
- ▶ Do all the links work?

Make changes if necessary. Ask others to check your prototypes. Use
their comments to make improvements.

Preview your pages on computers using different browsers, such
as Internet Explorer and Netscape. Check that the pages work on
different sized monitors.

When you think you have a version that works, try to find test users
who are similar to your target audience. Collect their feedback in
an organised way. Activity 7.10 provides a suggested checklist for
collecting feedback.

Remember the production cycle:

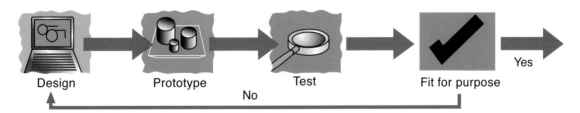

Design Prototype Test Fit for purpose Yes

No

> ## ▶▶Activity 7.10
>
> 1 **Choose suitable test users to look at your web pages for
>   the Bentley Charity Ball.**
> 2 **Collect feedback using the checklist provided.**
> 3 **Use the feedback to make improvements.**

Information leaflets

Not everyone has access to the internet. Many people prefer printed publications.

Leaflets can be posted, handed out or left in public places for people to pick up. Many organisations make information available in this way.

Sometimes an organisation will use a poster or flyer to attract attention and make further information available in a leaflet.

TALKING POINT 7.3

Look at each of these leaflets and discuss:
- ▶ *audience and purpose*
- ▶ *size of paper*
- ▶ *orientation — landscape or portrait?*
- ▶ *colours (full colour/two colour/black and white)*
- ▶ *number of folds*
- ▶ *layout and use of white space.*

Which leaflets do you think are the most effective and why? Remember any good ideas and use them in your own publications.

Planning

Start by deciding:

- ▶ **who** the target audience is
- ▶ **why** the leaflet is needed
- ▶ **where** it will be distributed
- ▶ **what** information it must contain
- ▶ **how** you will go about producing it.

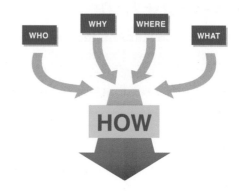

Designing a leaflet

What paper size and how many folds?

Most leaflets are printed on A4 paper and then folded. You should decide exactly how you will do this before you design the rest of the leaflet.

Sketch some designs on paper and find out what works best. Will you have a two-fold or three-fold leaflet?

A4 can be folded to make A5 leaflets like this

A4 can be folded twice to produce a leaflet like this

Choosing colours

Stick to simple colour combinations. Try to relate the colours to the theme of the leaflet. For example, if the leaflet is about an activity day for young children, the colours will probably be bright and cheerful.

Choose your background and foreground colours carefully. Print your leaflet to make sure that all text is easy to read. What you see on screen won't always look the same in print.

Greens and earthy colours will suit a leaflet about a country park but are not so effective for a leaflet about children's toys

Using text

Fonts

Choose fonts that are easy to read when printed.

Generally all the text should be the same font, except possibly the headings. Use different text sizes, bold or underline to show how important each piece of text is.

Alignment

Align text and other components to make the leaflet neat and ordered.

Remember to check that the alignment works when the leaflet is folded.

Bullets

Bullets are useful for making lists easier to read. Lists with bullets should be aligned left.

Using images

Images are an essential part of most leaflets. They are especially important on the front cover.

Finding suitable images

Images printed on a leaflet will often be quite small. Bear this in mind when you are selecting or creating them on screen.

Don't forget that you must have permission to use images if they belong to someone else.

Deciding where to put them

Position an image near the text that goes with it. Leave some space around the image. Don't have the text too close.

Make sure the folds will not spoil the image.

Making sure they are good enough quality

Images that display clearly on screen won't necessarily look so good when printed. This is particularly true for photographs. Use images that have good resolution. If you are capturing images using a digital camera, set it to medium or high resolution.

Using tables

Insert a table into a leaflet whenever a grid of rows and columns will make the information clearer.

Headings and sub-headings

Use headings and sub-headings to introduce each section of text. Make sure that the format and style of headings is consistent.

> **TALKING POINT 7.4**
>
> *Look at the sample leaflets on this page. Discuss the use of colour, images and text style.*

Layout

The layout of your leaflet will depend on how you decide to fold the paper. Make sure the layout is clear when the leaflet is folded.

White space and margins

Don't cram too much into your leaflet. Use white space to separate different sections and make the leaflet easy to read. Set the margins so you have space around the edges, but don't make them too big.

Creating a leaflet

Can I do this?

Using word processing or desktop publishing tools, make sure you can:

Use columns	Format text
Wrap text	Capture images
Import and position images	Align text and images
Crop and resize images	Use bullets
Change margins	Change colours
Use text boxes	Use lines and borders
Create a table	Insert page numbers

▸▸ Activity 7.11

In pairs, produce a checklist of things to consider when designing an information leaflet.

▸▸ Activity 7.12

You have to produce an information leaflet for THE PROJECT. Read the brief carefully and make a start on the design.

Ask yourself:

▸ How will you fold the leaflet?
▸ Which font styles and colours will you use?
▸ Will your design work?

Tackling THE PROJECT

P

In Chapter 6 you produced publications that attracted attention. The aim of this part of **THE PROJECT** is to produce an information point and leaflet that make information available.

As you work on your publications:

▶ keep reminding yourself of the audience and purpose

▶ make sure that it is easy for users to find their way round. Remember that you will not be there to explain things.

Information point

You have already:

▶ produced a storyboard (see Activity 7.7)

▶ created a homepage (see Activity 7.9).

Now create the rest of your information point. Check the 'Information point' section of **THE PROJECT** brief. Make sure that you do all that it asks.

Leaflet

Look at the work you did on the design of your leaflet (see Activity 7.12). Now read the 'Leaflet' section of **THE PROJECT** brief again. When you are happy with your design, create your leaflet and complete the rest of the activities for this section.

Note: For details of acceptable file formats see Chapter 9.

8 Getting the message across – targeting a known audience

Sometimes you know exactly who will read your publication, why it is needed and how it must be presented. For example, if you write a job application, it will be read by an employer (**who**), it is needed to apply for a job (**why**) and it will probably sent through the post or by email. Or, you might give a presentation to other students (**who**), its purpose could be to promote a new dance club (**why**) and it would take place in the school hall (**where**).

Knowing all this can make things easier for you. However, when you know who the audience is, you must make the publication really suitable for them. They will expect you to get it spot on.

There are important decisions to be made. Will the audience prefer a paper-based or onscreen publication? What style will be most suitable? What do they know already? What information do they need?

In this chapter you will learn how to target individuals and groups by:

▶ *designing publications, including formal letters, presentations, newsletters and reports*

▶ *creating prototypes for testing and feedback*

▶ *ensuring that final publications are fit for purpose*

Formal letters

A letter creates an immediate impression of what the sender is like. A sloppy letter creates the impression of a sloppy person.

To make a good impression you must produce a good letter.

Standard components of a formal letter

You must make sure that a letter includes all the standard components. An example is shown below. Make sure all text is left aligned, apart from the sender's address.

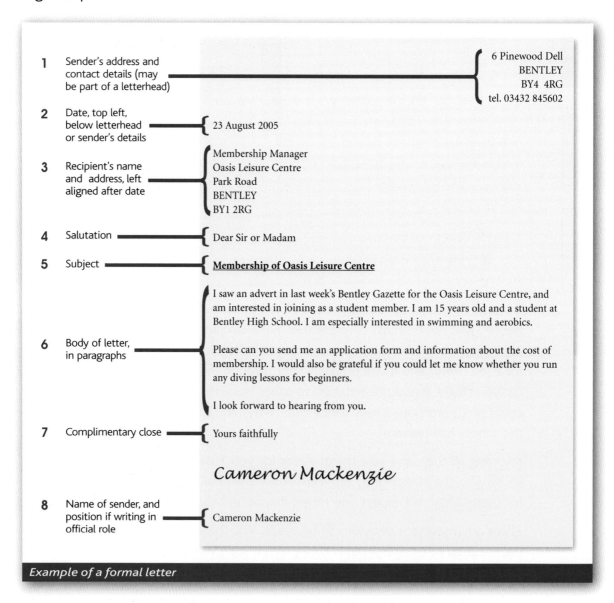

1 Sender's address and contact details (may be part of a letterhead)

> 6 Pinewood Dell
> BENTLEY
> BY4 4RG
> tel. 03432 845602

2 Date, top left, below letterhead or sender's details

> 23 August 2005

3 Recipient's name and address, left aligned after date

> Membership Manager
> Oasis Leisure Centre
> Park Road
> BENTLEY
> BY1 2RG

4 Salutation

> Dear Sir or Madam

5 Subject

> **Membership of Oasis Leisure Centre**

6 Body of letter, in paragraphs

> I saw an advert in last week's Bentley Gazette for the Oasis Leisure Centre, and am interested in joining as a student member. I am 15 years old and a student at Bentley High School. I am especially interested in swimming and aerobics.
>
> Please can you send me an application form and information about the cost of membership. I would also be grateful if you could let me know whether you run any diving lessons for beginners.
>
> I look forward to hearing from you.

7 Complimentary close

> Yours faithfully

> *Cameron Mackenzie*

8 Name of sender, and position if writing in official role

> Cameron Mackenzie

Example of a formal letter

1 **Sender's details**. If you are sending a personal letter, you should include your address and contact details in the top right corner of the letter. Do not include your name. Don't use punctuation in the address.

2 **Date of letter.** The date should come at the top left or right, below the sender's details. This must include the month as text and the year.

✓ 4 April 2006 ✗ 4/4/06 ✗ Monday, 4th April 2006

3 **Recipient's details.** This should include the full name of the person receiving the letter. Only use a title if you know what it should be.

✓ Mrs S Johnson ✓ Sheelagh Johnson ✗ Sheelagh

Include the recipient's full postal address, including postcode. Put the town in capital letters. Notice there is no punctuation in the address.

4 **Salutation.** For a formal letter, you can use the person's title if you know what it is – Mr, Mrs, Ms, Miss, Dr, etc. Do not include the first name or initial as well as the title.

✓ Dear Mrs Johnson

✗ Dear Mrs S Johnson

✗ Dear Mrs Sheelagh Johnson

If you don't know the title, but you know the full name you can use this:

✓ Dear Sheelagh Johnson

but not this:

✗ Dear S Johnson

If you do not know the person's name, use Dear Sir/Madam.

5 **Subject.** This says what the letter is about. It should come after the salutation and before the main body of the letter. It can be bold or underlined.

6 **Body of letter.** This is set out in paragraphs with correct punctuation. Leave a blank line between paragraphs.

7 **Complimentary close.** This will depend on the opening salutation. If you have used a person's name, it should be Yours sincerely. If you have used Sir or Madam, it should be Yours faithfully.

8 **Sender's name and position.** After leaving space for a signature, you should type your name on one line. If you are writing on behalf of an organisation add your job title below your name.

Enclosures

You will often see 'Enc' at the end of a letter. It is short for 'Enclosure' and means that another document is enclosed in the envelope.

Writing letters for an organisation or business

Most organisations use a standard letterhead on all their communications. If you are given a letterhead to use you must *not* change it in any way even if you don't like it! All text that you add should come below the letterhead.

Examples of letterheads

TALKING POINT 8.1

Why is it important to follow the rules for a formal letter?

▸▸Activity 8.1

Open this folder, which contains examples of formal letters. Some are from private individuals and some are from companies.

Compare them. How do they differ? Look at the position of the standard components.

▸▸ Activity 8.2

Create a formal letter using the components shown in the table.
Click here to do this as a drag and drop exercise.

Yours sincerely	25 February 2005
I have enclosed a copy of my updated CV as requested and I look forward to seeing you on 8 March.	Dear Mr Bluestone
Enc	Further to our meeting last Thursday, I am writing to accept your offer of a work experience placement in your office next month.
I will report to the post room on Monday, 8 March 2005, at 8.30 am for my induction programme with Miss Shaw. Thank you for sending a copy of your staff handbook. I will make sure that I understand all the procedures before I start. I have read the office dress code and understand that I must not wear jeans or trainers.	Mr J Bluestone 17 Moorside Green Road Blythe Bridge STOKE ON TRENT ST21 4RF
25 Stoke Place Hanley BENTLEY BT25 5RP Telephone: 09782 3746910 E-mail: maggiesalt@etinternet.com	Margaret Salt (Miss)
	WORK EXPERIENCE

TALKING POINT 8.2

Look at these letters. Do they have all the correct components?
How do they differ? Are they fit for purpose?

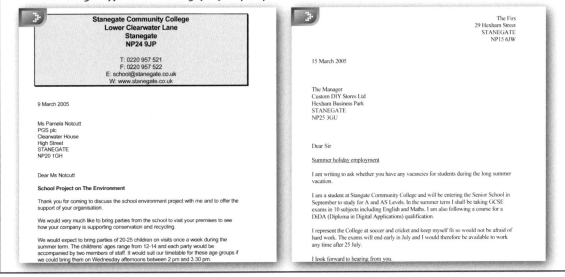

Proofreading

You must always proofread your work. Don't rely on the spellchecker.

If you skipped Activity 6.7 on page 93 you may like to do it now. It will remind you how the spellchecker can mislead you.

Once you think your letter is perfect, print off a copy and check it again.

Ask someone else to read it and give you feedback. Make corrections and check again.

Park Road
BENTLEY
BY1 2RG
Tel. 03432 724454

Please insert name and address of member here

~~25 May~~ *1 June* 2005

Dear Member

Oasis Leisure Centre – Swimming ~~facitilities~~ *facilities*

I'm delighted to inform that we are improving our swimming facilities.
- The changing rooms will be refurbished and more large lockers will be added. *Please insert a full stop here*
- New more powerful showers will be installed.

So that this work can be accomplished. *the pool will be closed for three weeks from 1 to 21 July, inclusive.* *Please insert comma as indicated and note that highlighted section should be Bold not Italic.*

A test user has looked at this letter and made notes

Is a letter fit for purpose?

Check:

- ▶ sender's contact details
- ▶ date
- ▶ body text
- ▶ spelling and grammar
- ▶ recipient's contact details
- ▶ salutation
- ▶ complimentary close (e.g. Yours sincerely)
- ▶ use of fonts.

Save this checklist. Use it when checking your own work. Offer it to test users to help them check your work.

▶▶ Activity 8.3

This letter was printed in the local newpaper.

The manager of the leisure centre has asked you to write a formal reply to send to the editor of the newspaper.

Open the full brief and read it carefully.

Use the checklist to make sure that your letter is fit for purpose and get feedback.

NEW SKI-SLOPE

SIR – I see that the Oasis Leisure Centre has started to build a dry ski slope. Its construction involves the demolition of the old barn that until recently housed the Bentley Gallery, and the felling of several well established trees.

Having recently visited friends who live near another ski centre, I can also promise that local residents will be subjected to continuous noise while the chairlifts are in use.

What was the council thinking of when it accepted such a proposal?

Tamsin Whetstone
Bentley

TALKING POINT 8.3

*As part of **THE PROJECT** you need to write a formal letter. Look at the details and discuss what points you could include for each letter.*

▸▸Activity 8.4

1 Decide which letter you will respond to. Make a list or draw a mindmap of the points you want to include in your reply. Look back at the notes you made in Chapter 2 to help you.
2 Write a paragraph for each point.
3 Use these paragraphs to create a formal letter. Make sure it includes all the necessary components. You can refer to the checklist to help you.

▸▸Activity 8.5

Work in groups to proofread each other's letters and discuss whether they are fit for purpose. Use the checklist provided above and the Mark Alert in **THE PROJECT** to help you.

Reports

Oh no, not reports! Reports are boring

Reports provide detailed information for people who need it.

Reports can easily be boring for the reader. Your challenge is to create reports that are attractive, useful and easy to read.

TALKING POINT 8.4

When might it be useful to use a report? Can you think of some examples? Who is the audience in each case? What is the purpose?
Now open the folder and look at the examples. Who is the target audience in each case? What do they aim to do? Are they fit for purpose?

Who, why, where, what, how?

Before you even think about designing a report, you need to know:

▶ how the report will be distributed — by post, at a meeting, etc

▶ whether there are other publications to go with it, such as a presentation

▶ what content must go in the report

▶ how many pages it will be

▶ how it will be produced and what software will be used.

Designing and creating a report

Reports consist mainly of text. You need to design them carefully for them to be effective. You can use what you know about designing posters and flyers to help you design reports. Go back and look at Chapter 6 again if you need to.

▶▶ Activity 8.6

The manager of the Oasis Youth Club in Bentley wants you to produce a report to accompany a presentation he is giving.

1 Read the briefing document.
2 In groups, decide which text goes in which of the following sections:
   ▶ what the youth club does and why it is successful
   ▶ why the club needs more money and how it would spend it.
3 Decide which text you will use, and in what order.

Can I do this?

Using word processing tools, make sure you can:

Format text

Align text

Wrap text

Paper size

Select the paper size. Most reports are printed on A4.

Which colours?

It is best to stick to black and white for text. Colour on charts and images make the reports more attractive. If you decide to print the report in black and white, make sure that the charts are clear when printed.

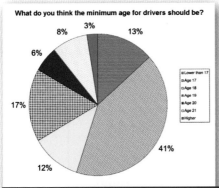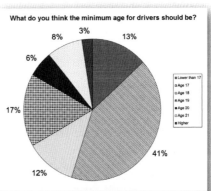

This chart is clear in colour and black and white

Fonts

▶ Choose a font that is easy to read when printed.

▶ Choose the size according to the importance of the text.

▶ Make sure that all the sizes are legible when printed.

▶ All the text should be in the same font.

▶ Make text bold, underlined or increase its size to show it is a heading.

▶ Don't use word art in formal reports.

This is not the way to get your report taken seriously

Choose a clear font	Choose a clear font	Choose a clear font
Choose a clear font	Choose a clear font	**Choose a clear font**

Some fonts are clearer than others

Headings and subheadings

Reports are often mostly text. They are easier to read if they are broken down into sections that can be read one at a time. Headings are in bold or a bigger text size.

Text alignment

Text should be left aligned.

This text is left aligned. This makes it easier to read. Always use left-aligned text in reports. It is much neater than other ways of aligning. Have a look!	This text is centred. It is not suitable for reports as it looks messy. If you want your report to look professional, don't centre your text.	This text is right aligned. Don't align your text like this in a report. It's difficult to read, isn't it?

Different ways of aligning text

▶▶ Activity 8.7

1 Choose which font you will use for the report for the youth club manager.

2 Create headings for your report. Use different text sizes and styles to show which text is most important. Align your text sensibly.

Can I do this?

Using word processing tools, make sure you can:

Use bullets
Create a numbered list

Bullets

Bullets can be used to make a list of points easier to read. Make sure that all the bullets in a list are consistent and in line.

During the day participants can try out lots of activities:

- Abseiling
- Orienteering
- Canoeing
- Disco dancing
- Swimming
- Beginners' snowboarding

The choice is theirs.

Numbered lists

If a list is in a particular order then it will make more sense to number the points rather than use bullets.

Results of girls' 100m race

1 Janice Watson
2 Aisha Khan
3 Cheryl Penn
4 Kate Roberts
5 Kelly Dodd
6 Angela Cheung
7 Sharika Maheswaran

▶▶ Activity 8.8

Look at any lists that appear in your report for the youth club manager. Decide whether they should be numbered or bulleted. Insert any necessary numbers or bullets.

Can I do this?

Using word processing tools, make sure you can:

Import and position images
Crop and resize images
Change margins
Use text boxes
Create a table
Insert page numbers

Using images

Images in reports should help get the message across. Often they will be diagrams or charts. Remember, only use them if they are appropriate.

When using images, check that the size and quality are suitable. Check that images look good when printed.

Make sure each image is correctly positioned. How will the text flow around each image?

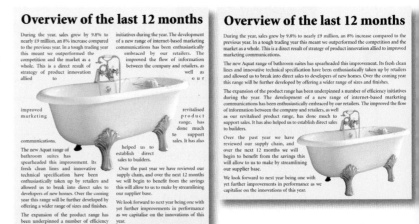

Which text has been spoilt by a badly placed image?

Using tables

If the information would be clearer in a grid of rows and columns, use a table.

Activity	Location	Age	Max per hour	Average per hour
Archery	Forest	10-16	12	4
Snowboard	Ski Slope	Over 10	20	20

Layout

Organise the information into manageable sections. Give each section a heading. Decide what you will include on each page and think about the position of images and text.

Try to space things out evenly. Make sure everything looks neat and tidy.

If there is more than one page, make sure that the page breaks are sensible.

White space

White space is important in all publications. Use plenty of white space to break up the text and balance the layout.

Margins and columns

Don't be afraid to change margins if this makes the report look better.

Page numbering

If a report is more than one page long, always insert page numbers.

▸▸Activity 8.9

1 Open the image folder for the report for the youth club manager. Choose some appropriate images to go with the text.
2 Decide what text and images will go on each page.
3 Insert the images. Crop or resize them if necessary.
4 Check that you have enough white space and that your layout is clear and tidy. Make adjustments if necessary.
5 Add page numbers to your report.

Keep on checking!

Check prototype versions of your report by asking the following questions:

▸ Are there any spelling or grammar mistakes?

▸ Is the text easy to understand?

▸ Is the style suitable and consistent?

▸ Is the layout clear?

Don't forget about the production cycle. Keep going back to the design until you are sure that it is fit for purpose.

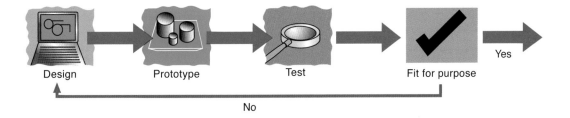

TALKING POINT 8.5

In earlier chapters we have given you a number of checklists to make checking and testing publications easier. Discuss what you might include in a checklist for testing a report.

▸▸Activity 8.10

1 In pairs, write a checklist for testing reports. Give your checklist to another pair and ask for feedback. Make any necessary changes.
2 Ask test users to look at the report you created for the youth club manager. Ask them to give you feedback using the checklist. Make any necessary changes.

Database reports

In Chapter 5 you learned how to search a database and sort the information you extracted. In this section you will learn how to produce database reports that get the message across effectively.

This is part of a report taken from the FILMS database you explored in Chapter 5. Is it clear what the report tells us? What do you think the report is for?

Query1

Serial Numbe	Title	Ratin	Category	Sales/r	Price	released
R108	Home Alone III	PG	Comedy	Rental	£1.99	1997
R114	The Wedding Date	PG	Comedy	Rental	£1.99	2005
R116	Ghostbusters	PG	Comedy	Rental	£2.99	1984
S110	A Cinderella Story	PG	Comedy	Sales	£9.99	2004
S111	Groundhog Day	PG	Comedy	Sales	£11.99	1993
R119	Back to the Future	PG	Comedy	Rental	£3.99	1985

TALKING POINT 8.6

The database report above was supposed to show mid-price children's comedy films for sale. How would you improve the report? Would you include different information?

Wizards are not magic

The report above was produced using a wizard. Wizards are there to help you but they will not do everything for you. Don't just click 'next' and hope it will turn out okay. You have to customise your reports.

Customising a report

Here is part of another report from the FILMS database. The author used a wizard, but also customised the report.

The best action films for hire

Title	Rating	Price
Charlie's Angels	15	£2.99
Pirates of the Caribbean	12	£2.99
Mission Impossible	PG	£3.99
Mission Impossible II	15	£2.99
Batman Begins	12	£4.99
Batman	PG	£1.99
Batman Returns	PG	£3.99
The Island	15	£1.99
Serenity	15	£2.99
King Kong	12	£2.99
Jurassic Park III	PG	£3.99

TALKING POINT 8.7

Why is this report more useful than the example on page 124? Would you do anything else to improve it?

Choosing fields

You don't need to include all fields in the database in every report. For example, in a report on rental films, you don't need to include the Sales/Rental field as all the films will be rental. Only include relevant information.

TALKING POINT 8.8

*Look at the MEALS database for **THE PROJECT**. What fields would you include in reports on the following:*
- *items for vegetarians*
- *special meals for diabetics*
- *desserts only*

Heading

This should make it clear what the report it about. Don't let the wizard do it for you.

Column headings

The wizard will use the field names from the database. Sometimes these will only be clear to the person who created the database. Customise them to make sure they are clear to everybody.

Layout

Check the spacing of the columns. This can be a problem if you have a right aligned field next to the left aligned field.

Footers

You can use page footers to enter details of the author, date of report etc. Be careful if you are using Microsoft Access. This has two different kinds of footer. The report footer will print after the last record, not at the bottom of the page.

Don't forget to check!

Show your report to someone who has not been working on it. They will tell you if things don't make sense.

Can I do this?

Using database tools make sure you can:

Create a report

Customise a report

▶▶**Activity 8.11**

Produce the three database reports for The Project that you planned in Talking Point 8.8.

Presentations

Most presentations are designed for a specific audience. They are likely to be gathered in one place to hear something that is useful to them.

Who is it for?

Ask yourself:

Who will be listening to your presentation?

Why do they need to be there?

How much do they already know?

What style of language is most suitable?

Why is it needed?

What is the purpose of the presentation?

Is it to persuade people, explain something or impress people?

The key message

A good presentation always has a key message. The audience should know what the key message is within the first 15 seconds.

The importance of the presenter

Web pages and information points have to be self-explanatory. The designer is not there to explain them to users.

Presentations are quite different. The presenter is there to explain things, while the slides provide a summary of what is being said.

Alternative Energy

An insight into what is going on in the world today

- Welcome
- Presentation: encourage councillors to look at ways of motivating young people
- Shows results of survey carried out on 50 teenagers.
- Gives recommendations towards helping teenagers create a better future.

Most presentation software allows you to enter the speaker notes below the slide so that you can print out pages like this

Slides and speaker notes

Presentations are made up of two distinct parts:

▶ the slides

▶ the notes to help the speaker remember what to say.

The time limit

Usually the presenter and the meeting organiser agree the time limit in advance.

Good presentations never run on beyond the time limit. Audiences tend to lose concentration after about 15 minutes, so the best presentations are shorter than this.

Designing and creating a presentation

Storyboarding

Storyboards are useful when designing presentations.

Each slide should have a distinct purpose and message, but the presentation should still flow from beginning to end.

A storyboard will help you to decide:

▶ how many slides you need

▶ the order of the slides

▶ what components will appear on each slide.

Use your storyboard to discuss your ideas with fellow students and get feedback.

Choosing components

Too many presentations suffer from silly sound effects, boring clip art, too many colours and fonts and too much information on cramped slides. Keep it simple! Remember that people at the back of the room need to be able to see everything on the slides too.

TALKING POINT 8.9

Look at this presentation. It is full of deliberate mistakes. How many can you spot?

> ### Alternative Energy
>
> An insight into what is going on in the world today

Can I do this?

Using presentation tools, make sure you can:

Create slides
Create and use a master slide
Change colours
Import and position images
Align text and images
Crop and resize images

Using text

Imagine that you are listening to the key message. Which slide would you rather see behind the speaker?

When creating slides:

▶ use short, snappy bullets

▶ stick to a few points per slide

▶ avoid writing whole words in capitals

▶ experiment with different fonts and sizes – try them out using a projector and screen.

You all have children in year 9 and I know that you are concerned that we are starting a new ICT course from September. I think that by the end of this 30 minute presentation you will be as confident as we are that your children are lucky to be the first students to benefit from studying DiDA. In fact, I think you may well find yourself asking when you can sign up!

What makes DiDA special?

Using images

Make sure that any images are relevant and send out the right message. Use cartoons and clip art with extra care. They can look unprofessional.

If you can't find something suitable, create your own images with a digital camera or by drawing them.

Which image gives out the right message?

Can I do this?

Using presentation tools, make sure you can:

Use lines and borders   **Include animation**

Include sound   **Create transitions**

Insert links

Using graphs and charts

Use graphs and charts to communicate numerical information, especially when there are comparisons to be made.

Using other multimedia components

Presentation tools allow us to use sound and animation. It is easy to get carried away and use them too much. Only use them occasionally, for instance, when you want to emphasise a point.

▶ **Sound:** Use sound only if it improves the quality of the presentation. Check that the equipment can play sound clearly.

▶ **Animation:** This allows you to make text and objects move. Select just a few types of animation and stick to them throughout a presentation. Don't have things flying from all directions, or your audience will be distracted.

▶ **Links and buttons:** These can be included in slides to allow the presenter to jump to other slides or files. For example, in a presentation on web page design, the presenter might want to link to an example of a website.

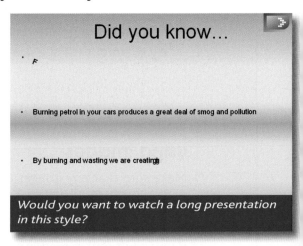

Did you know...

· F

· Burning petrol in your cars produces a great deal of smog and pollution

· By burning and wasting we are creating

Would you want to watch a long presentation in this style?

Choosing colours

Try out different colours to see what looks best on screen.

What makes DiDA special?

What makes DiDA special?

What makes DiDA special?

What makes DiDA special?

Consistency

Make sure all the slides in a presentation have some common features, such as the same colours, the same font, or even an image that appears on every slide.

You can use a master slide to make sure your presentation is consistent. This is a template that contains the features you want to use on every slide. At Level 1 the use of a master slide is optional.

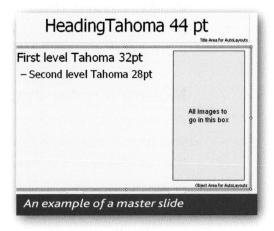

An example of a master slide

Transitions

Transitions control how the presentation moves from one slide to the next. Look at this example. Too many different types of transition have been used here.

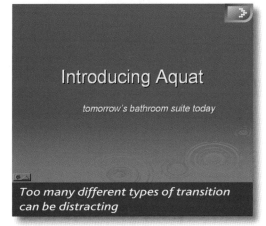

Too many different types of transition can be distracting

Proofreading

Spelling mistakes always create a poor impression.

On a slide they will be very big and everyone in the room will see them. Check, check, and check again!

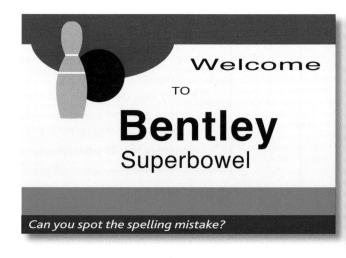

Welcome TO **Bentley** Superbowel

Can you spot the spelling mistake?

Making it more than just a slide show

The presenter is the most important part of a presentation. Practise your presentation. Sound enthusiastic about what you are saying. Never just read the slides out. Make sure that you know what you are going to say for each slide. Look at the audience when you are speaking and don't keep turning round to look at the slides behind you. Avoid just reading the speaker notes.

> **TALKING POINT 8.11**
>
> *Look at the Mark Alert for the presentation in THE PROJECT. Discuss each item on the list and check that you understand it. Discuss how you will test your prototype presentation.*

> **▶▶ Activity 8.14**
>
> 1 Using your storyboard, create a presentation for THE PROJECT.
> 2 Check it carefully yourself. Then ask a classmate for feedback. Don't forget to record the feedback you are given. Use it to make improvements to your presentation.

Other uses of presentations

A presentation can be set up to run by itself. This method can be used to provide information in a public area, such as the foyer of a leisure centre. Passers-by can stop and watch.

Newsletters

First impressions

A newsletter is not the same as an information leaflet. People read an information leaflet because they want specific information.

A newsletter is optional reading - people do not need to read it. If it is not designed well, they probably won't bother. A newsletter needs to be attractive and interesting.

Once again, ask yourself:

▶ **Who** it is for? How old are they? What sort of writing style will appeal to them? How much (or how little) do they already know?

▶ **Why** have a newsletter? What is its purpose. Notice how the Tyntesfield News has a sub-heading 'Sharing what we do'. This makes its purpose clear.

▶ **What** should go in it? Concentrate on what the audience will want to read, not on what you want to write. When you plan the pages, make sure that important items stand out.

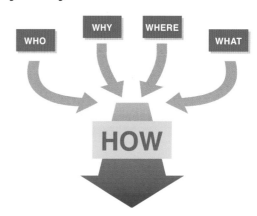

TALKING POINT 8.12

Look at these newsletters. Can you describe

▶ *Audience and purpose*
▶ *Number and size of pages*
▶ *Title*
▶ *Content*
▶ *Colours*
▶ *Use of images*
▶ *Writing style*
▶ *Layout?*

Designing a newsletter

Although a leaflet has a different purpose to a newsletter, they have many similar features. Rather than repeat all the information here you should refer to Chapter 7.

Common features include:

▶ Paper size and folds   ▶ Colours

▶ Font types and styles   ▶ Images

▶ Alignment and bullets.

Pages

You will need to consider how many pages you will need – a newsletter is likely to have at least 4 sides. Also what page size? A4 or A5 are popular choices.

Choosing a focus

Every page should give the reader a clear reason to stop and look. This focus could be a catchy title or an image. Build a page around this focus. The front page needs to be particularly appealing.

TALKING POINT 8.13

Look at these newsletters. What catches your attention? What is the focus of each page?

Columns

If you use columns, make sure they are balanced – roughly the same amount in each.

Choosing your software

Desktop publishing software seems the obvious choice. However, word processing software can also produce excellent newsletters. For Unit 1, you can use any suitable software.

Creating a newsletter

Can I do this?

Using word processing or desktop publishing tools, make sure you can:

Use columns	**Use bullets**
Format text	**Change margins**
Align text	**Change colours**
Wrap text	**Use text boxes**
Capture images	**Use lines and borders**
Import and position images	**Create and use a table**
Align text and images	**Insert page numbers**
Crop and resize images	

TALKING POINT 8.14

Discuss a possible newsletter for your class to produce. Who will it be for? What will its purpose be? What will go in it? Plan what might go on each page. Decide how many pages it will have and what the focus for each page might be.

▶▶ Activity 8.15

As a group, design and produce the newsletter as discussed in Talking Point 8.14.

Testing, testing!

Create a prototype of your newsletter and check it carefully for:

▶ mistakes

▶ readability & writing style

▶ consistency

▶ sensible use of images

▶ layout and use of white space

▶ impact of front cover.

▶▶ Activity 8.16

Test your newsletter by asking test users from the target audience for comments. Keep a record of their feedback and use it to make changes to improve the publication.

Tackling **THE PROJECT**

Now it's time to complete the publications that target a known audience.

Formal letter

You have already written your letter and got feedback from your test users (see Activities 8.4 and 8.5). Now complete the rest of the 'Formal letter' section of **THE PROJECT** brief.

Survey report

Read the 'Survey report' section of **THE PROJECT** brief. Complete all of the activities described.

Database report

Read the 'Database reports' section of **THE PROJECT** brief. In Chapter 5 you created the searches. Now you need to produce reports using your search results.

You have already created reports for three of your searches (see Talking Point 8.8 and Activity 8.11). Now create reports for the other searches and complete the rest of this section. Don't forget the two searches of your own.

Presentation

You have already done a lot of the work for your presentation (see Talking Points 8.10 and 8.11 and Activities 8.13 and 8.14). Read through the 'Presentation' section of **THE PROJECT** brief again and complete any remaining work.

Note: For details of acceptable file formats see Chapter 9.

9 Producing an eportfolio

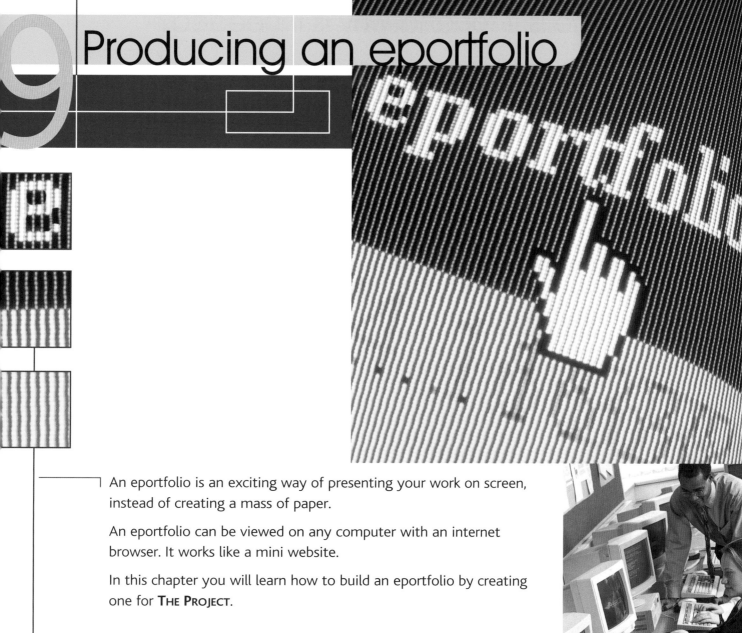

An eportfolio is an exciting way of presenting your work on screen, instead of creating a mass of paper.

An eportfolio can be viewed on any computer with an internet browser. It works like a mini website.

In this chapter you will learn how to build an eportfolio by creating one for **THE PROJECT**.

In this chapter, ou will learn how to design and build an eportfolio by:

- ► *choosing the content*
- ► *creating a folder structure to store the evidence*
- ► *designing the web pages*
- ► *converting the files*
- ► *building the eportfolio*
- ► *testing that it works*

Who is it for and why is it needed?

When you do the real SPB, the audience for your eportfolio will be the moderator. The purpose will be to show off what you have achieved during your work on the SPB. To give you some practice you are going to create an eportfolio for **THE PROJECT**.

With any eportfolio, the aim is to impress people, so it has to be well designed.

What should go in it?

Keep reminding yourself of the audience. Nobody wants to see an eportfolio padded out with any old work, especially not a moderator. It's quality, not quantity that counts.

TALKING POINT 9.1

THE PROJECT is similar to a real SPB but without the project planning.

Imagine that you need to submit an eportfolio of your work on **THE PROJECT** to a moderator. What does the moderator need to see? How can you create the right impression?

▸▸Activity 9.1

Look at the 'eportfolio' section of **THE PROJECT** and find the checklist for what you should include in your eportfolio. Have you got everything you need?

You will probably not have a project review yet. You will produce this later.

Designing an eportfolio structure

The eportfolio consists of a series of web pages. Each page will have links to some of your evidence. We will look at one possible structure for an eportfolio for **THE PROJECT**. When you do the real SPB you can use a similar structure or design your own.

What matters is that the eportfolio is easy to use. A structure chart helps us to show how the eportfolio fits together.

Home page

Every eportfolio should have a **home page.** This is where you introduce yourself and make the user want to look at the rest. You must include links to allow the user to move around.

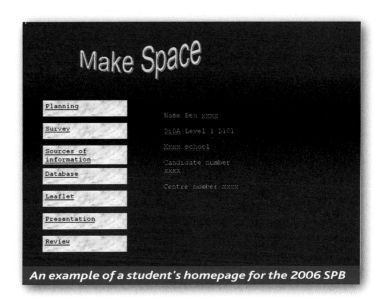

An example of a student's homepage for the 2006 SPB

Context pages

From the home page the user should be able to go to each main section of your eportfolio. Each section will be introduced by a **context page.** This will tell the user what evidence is in the section and include links to it.

Survey

This context page includes information about your survey and links to the evidence (the green boxes). You could have a separate context page for each file.

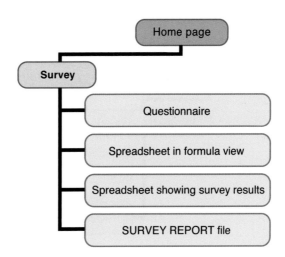

Database

This context page includes information about your database work and links to the evidence.

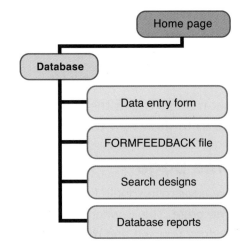

Publications

As there are so many publications in **THE PROJECT**, it is easier to split them into two sections. There is a context page for printed publications with links to the leaflet, report, poster, flyer and letter. There is a separate context page with links for the onscreen publications.

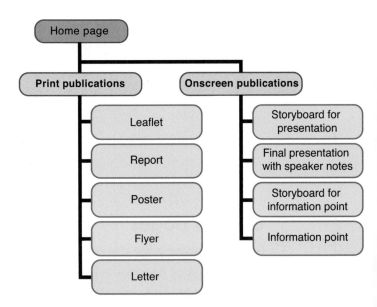

Research and review

This context page links to your supporting evidence. For **THE PROJECT** this is evidence of your research and your project review. For the real SPB you will also have a project plan.

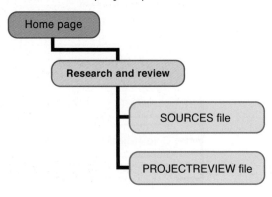

Now we can put all this together in one chart that shows the structure of the whole eportfolio. Turn to pages 142 and 143 to see this chart.

TALKING POINT 9.2

Make sure that you understand the complete structure chart on the next two pages. Does it include all the evidence on the checklist you looked at in Activity 9.1?

▶▶Activity 9.2

Copy the structure chart for your eportfolio. Check that it includes everything on the list. You can include the file names of your evidence if you want to. What links will you need on your navigation bar?

Navigation

When you design the navigation you decide what links are needed so that users can move around the eportfolio. It helps if the navigation is simple and consistent. One way to make sure of this is to use a navigation bar — more on this later.

Links to the different parts of your eportfolio should only appear on the home page or context pages. Do **not** put a link to the home page or any other part of the eportfolio in a publication. Imagine a user looking at your information point and seeing a button saying 'Back to eportfolio'. It would not make sense!

On the context page you can tell the user how to get out of a publication. For example, 'use the back button to return to this page'.

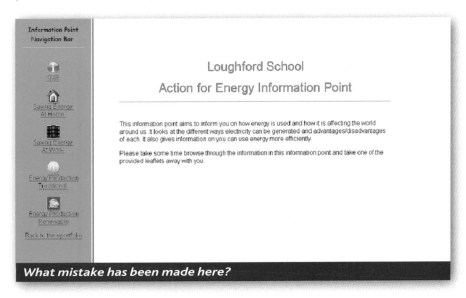

What mistake has been made here?

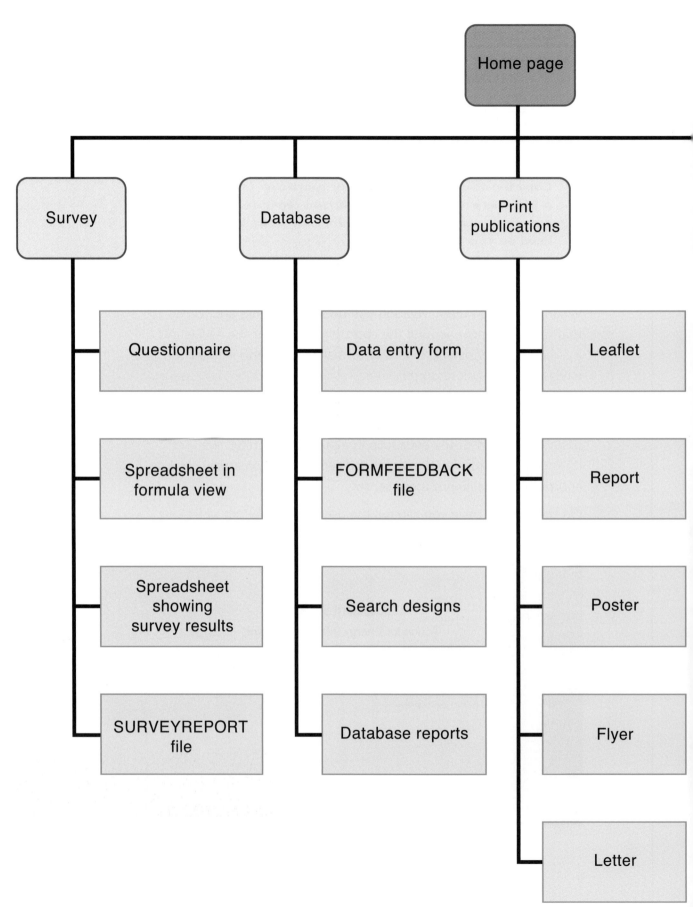

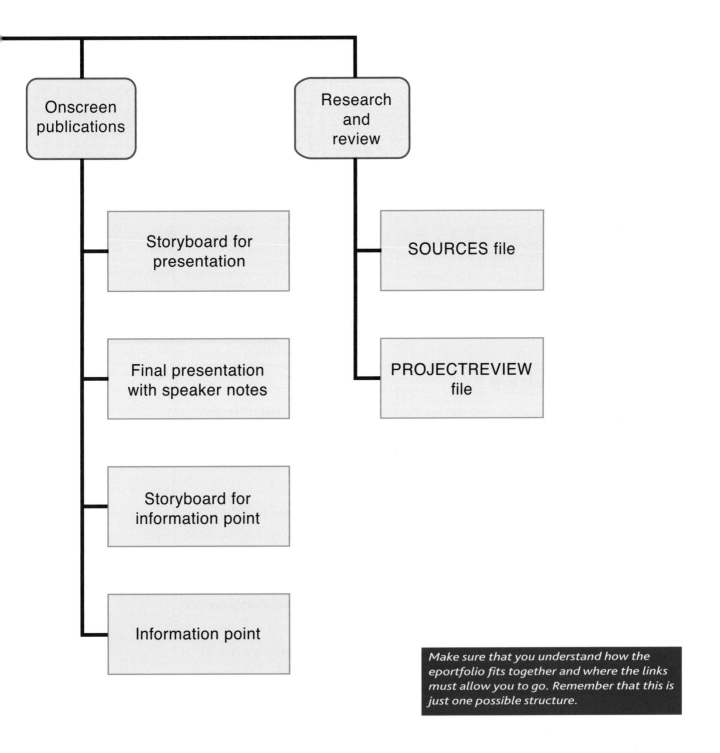

Onscreen
publications

Research
and
review

Storyboard for
presentation

SOURCES file

Final presentation
with speaker notes

PROJECTREVIEW
file

Storyboard for
information point

Information point

*Make sure that you understand how the
eportfolio fits together and where the links
must allow you to go. Remember that this is
just one possible structure.*

Designing the web pages

You must design each page of your eportfolio using a storyboard. How will users find their way around? How will you make it obvious to them?

Make it obvious where the links are

There are a number of ways of including links in the eportfolio.

▶ **Text** is a simple way to identify a link. The text should be underlined. For example, 'See what you think of my <u>presentation to club members</u>.'

▶ **Images and symbols** can be used to show links. Make sure they are relevant.

▶ **Buttons** perform an action when you click them. They can be text or images. Sometimes they change when you move over them. ▸ is an example of a button.

Examples of types of link

> ▶▶ **Activity 9.3**
>
> Explore your web authoring software and try out different types of link – text, images and buttons.

Consistency and navigation bars

You will make life much easier for the user if you place your links in the same position on every page of your eportfolio. This can be done using a navigation bar.

The bar can use text links, image links or buttons, but they should be the same on each page. Users soon get to know where things are on the bar because it is consistent.

The website for Wiltshire Farm Foods on the opposite page has a series of buttons across the top of the home page. On all the other pages there is a navigation bar on the left. This is the same on every page and allows you to move around without going back to the home page.

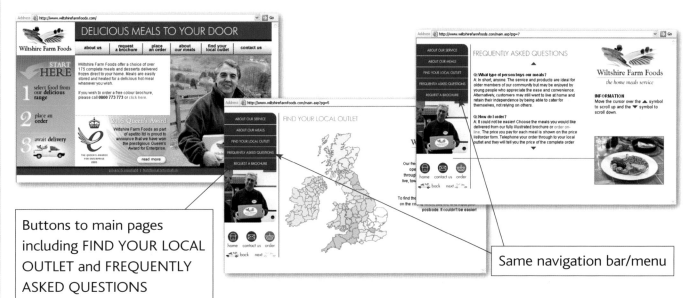

Buttons to main pages including FIND YOUR LOCAL OUTLET and FREQUENTLY ASKED QUESTIONS

Same navigation bar/menu

▶▶ Activity 9.4

1 **Check out the website for Wiltshire Farm Foods. What navigation features do you like on this site? Which features don't you like?**

2 **Have a look at the navigation bars on some other sites that you like to visit.**

3 **Sketch out a design for a navigation bar for your eportfolio for THE PROJECT. It should include a link to the context page for each section of the eportfolio as well as a link to the home page.**

The home page

The home page is the most important page in your eportfolio. Think of it as a shop window that makes people want to open the door and see what is inside.

Your home page must include:

▶ information about you

▶ a clear description of the purpose of the eportfolio

▶ links that enable the user to go to each section of the eportfolio.

Make the page attractive – use a *suitable* image that illustrates the content or purpose. Don't be tempted to include images just because you like them!

TALKING POINT 9.3

What makes a good home page for an eportfolio?

The context pages

Most of these pages are likely to include:

- ▶ the purpose of the section
- ▶ information about how you produced the evidence
- ▶ a link to each item of evidence and to the home page.

▶▶Activity 9.5

Before designing your eportfolio in detail, get a feel for what is involved by looking at some student eportfolios on the Edexcel website.

Storyboarding

Use a storyboard to design the pages for your eportfolio. You must decide:

- ▶ what will appear on each page
- ▶ the position of everything on each page
- ▶ how the navigation will look and where the links will go.

▶▶Activity 9.6

Create a storyboard for the pages of your eportfolio for The Project. Use the structure chart to help you and think about text, images and navigation (links).

Working in pairs, explain your storyboard to your partner and get their feedback. Make improvements where necessary.

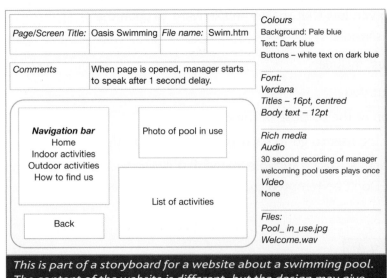

This is part of a storyboard for a website about a swimming pool. The content of the website is different, but the design may give you some ideas for your eportfolio storyboard.

Building an eportfolio

Can I do this?

Using web authoring tools, make sure you can:

Create a logical file structure

Convert files to other formats

Create web pages

Create a navigation bar

Insert links

Use text and images as links

Open a page or file in a new window

Folder structure

Now you have designed your eportfolio, it's time to make sure that it has a sensible folder structure and that all the files are in the right places.

Look at the example below.

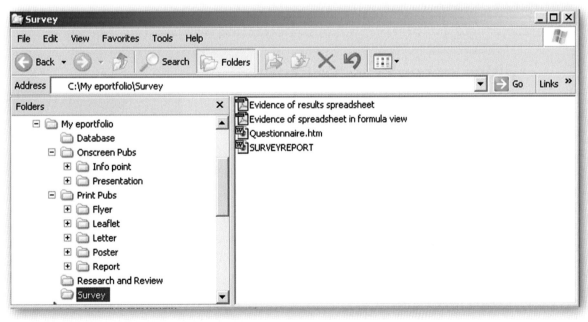

> ▶▶ **Activity 9.7**
>
> Create the folder structure for your eportfolio for THE PROJECT.
> Create this in your user area. Do not put the files in yet.

Moving evidence into your eportfolio

Once you are happy with your structure, you can *copy* the files into the correct folders. Some of the files may need to be converted into acceptable file formats.

Look at this screenshot. You will see that the folder called 'presentation' contains:

▶ the storyboard for a presentation

▶ the final version of a presentation

▶ the speaker notes.

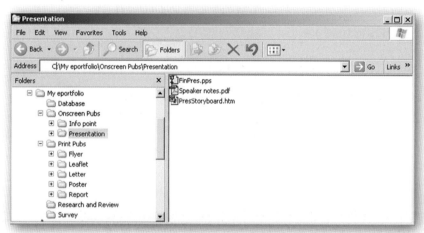

Using acceptable file formats

A message like this means that your computer cannot open the file because you do not have the right software.

If this happens when the moderator is looking at your eportfolio, it will be a serious problem.

This is why you are told which file formats are acceptable. For the SPB there is a list in the brief.

Only use file formats that are on the list.

| **TALKING POINT 9.4** |

How do you know what format a file is in? Can you explain why it is important to use the correct file formats for your eportfolio?

Free software and viewers

Sometimes it is possible to view files even though you don't have the software to create them. Windows Media Player is a good example – it allows you to listen to music and watch videos even if you cannot produce them yourself. This is why file formats such as wmv are allowed.

Creating acceptable file formats

You must check that each piece of evidence is in an acceptable file format before you include it in your eportfolio.

In many software applications you have the option to save files in different formats. Sometimes you may need to use a converter program to convert publications to acceptable formats.

This table gives the file formats that can currently be used in Unit 1 eportfolios.

File type	Used for
html, htm, xml	web pages, word processing, desktop publishing
txt	data sets, word processing
pdf	word processing, desktop publishing
swf	movies, presentations, screen recording
mov, avi, wmv	video
wav, midi, mp3	sound
jpg, png, gif, tif	images
pps, ppt	presentations, information points

▸▸ Activity 9.8

Open the file and save a copy as FORMATS in your user area. Use it to check that you only use formats that are on the list.

▸▸**Activity 9.9**

1 **Look at all the files you want to put in your eportfolio. Check that they are all in acceptable file formats.**
2 **Copy the necessary files into your eportfolio folders.**

You do not yet have a project review so you won't have a file for this.

Creating links that work

Your eportfolio will only work properly if you get all the links right. This is really important because other people will look at your eportfolio on their own computers.

It means making sure of three things:

▸ that you have all the files you need in the right folders inside your eportfolio structure

▸ that each link goes to the right file

▸ that you have used the right sort of link.

You know about the first one already. Now you are going to look at links.

Linking to the right file

When you link to each file, make sure you link to the version you have placed inside your eportfolio. You will probably have other copies on your system and versions with different file formats.

If the file you want to link to isn't in the right place, move it first, then create the link.

Using the right type of link

Using the right types of link can be tricky, but you can get help if you need it.

How you create your links will depend on what software you are using. In Macromedia Dreamweaver, for example, links to evidence files can be created by dragging or pointing to the file you want to link to.

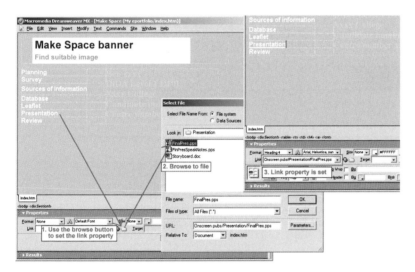

You can only be sure that your links are right by testing your eportfolio very carefully, including every single link on every page. Don't check one and assume the others will be okay.

▸▸ Activity 9.10

Open your web authoring software. Make sure that you understand how to create links for your eportfolio.

Testing your links

Testing on your own computer or the school network is not enough. Some types of link may only work on the machine you created the eportfolio on. That's not good enough. How will a moderator be able to see your publications if the links only work on your computer?

The important thing is that your links will work even when the eportfolio is viewed on another system.

It is vital that you test your eportfolio on another machine.

TALKING POINT 9.6

How will you make sure that your SPB eportfolio will work for the moderator?

What do you do if links don't work?

Look at the address for each link.

Does the file you have tried to link to actually exist in the folder? Is the filename correct?

What is wrong with this link?

If you see a folder in the link address which is not part of your eportfolio, something is wrong. The moderator's computer will not be able to find folders that are on your hard drive! Look out for folders such as 'My Documents'. If they are not inside your eportfolio structure, they should not be in the link.

It is a good idea to load your eportfolio onto another system, a standalone PC or laptop, and check that everything works as it should.

Getting the size right

For DiDA SPBs there will be a maximum size. If you submit an eportfolio that is bigger than this maximum, your work may not be accepted.

How do you find out the size of your eportfolio?

This will depend on the software you are using.

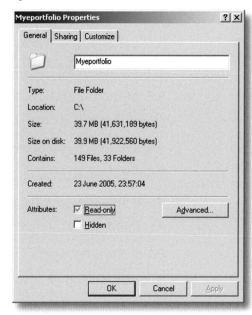

For example, in Windows Explorer, you can right click on any folder and select 'Properties'. This will display information about the size.

The maximum for a Unit 1 SPB is 15MB so this example is clearly way too big!

What do you do if your eportfolio is too big?

There are a number of ways you can make your eportfolio smaller.

Optimise the images

Image files are often very large. You can make the file size smaller reducing the resolution or by cropping them. Remember that resizing images will not help.

Change the file formats

Some file formats take up far more space than others. Look what happened when I saved the draft version of this chapter as a '.doc', a '.pdf' and an '.rtf'.

Chapter 9 Producing an eportfolio v4.doc	2,082 KB	Microsoft Word Document	05/05/2005 20:05
Chapter 9 Producing an eportfolio v4.pdf	404 KB	Adobe Acrobat Document	05/05/2005 20:05
Chapter 9 Producing an eportfolio v4.rtf	86,831 KB	Rich Text Format	05/05/2005 20:06

This is why rtf is not an acceptable file format for Unit 1 eportfolios!

The pdf format takes up the least space. It is a read-only format which means that it cannot be changed.

Leave things out

This is a bit drastic. But if all else fails, you will have to leave out things that are not absolutely necessary, such as images.

Prototyping and testing

Test your eportfolio to ensure that it works. In particular, test it on a standalone PC or laptop to make sure that all the links work.

Ask test users to see if they can find anything that does not work.

Check	Feedback
Is it suitable for a moderator?	
Is it the right size? Check the maximum in the brief.	
Are all the file formats acceptable?	
Does it include all the required evidence?	
Are any unnecessary files included?	
Does it have a good user interface?	
Is the home page effective?	
Are there any errors on the context pages?	
Do all the links work?	
Is it easy to find your way around?	
Are the images of good enough quality?	
Is all the text readable? (style, size, colour)	
Are all the web pages well designed?	
Are sources acknowledged?	
Are the context pages effective?	
Does it all work on a different system?	

Use the feedback to identify problems and make improvements.

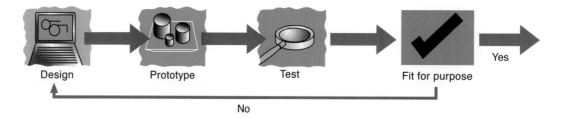

Design → Prototype → Test → Fit for purpose → Yes

No

▸▸Activity 9.11

Open the checklist. Add more questions and more space for comments if you think these are needed.

Creating an effective eportfolio

There is a lot to take in isn't there? But if you follow these steps, you should stay on track.

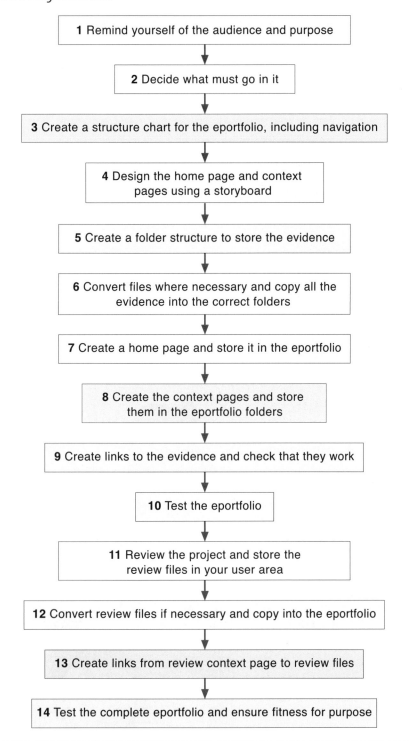

1 Remind yourself of the audience and purpose

2 Decide what must go in it

3 Create a structure chart for the eportfolio, including navigation

4 Design the home page and context pages using a storyboard

5 Create a folder structure to store the evidence

6 Convert files where necessary and copy all the evidence into the correct folders

7 Create a home page and store it in the eportfolio

8 Create the context pages and store them in the eportfolio folders

9 Create links to the evidence and check that they work

10 Test the eportfolio

11 Review the project and store the review files in your user area

12 Convert review files if necessary and copy into the eportfolio

13 Create links from review context page to review files

14 Test the complete eportfolio and ensure fitness for purpose

▸▸Activity 9.12

Before you move on to Tackling The Project, check through steps 1 to 6 and make sure that you are happy with what you have done so far.

Tackling THE PROJECT

Your eportfolio is nearly finished!

Read the 'eportfolio' section of THE PROJECT brief. Keep this in mind as you move on to steps 7 to 10 of the chart on page 155.

Ask yourself:

Have I got all the evidence I need?

Check that you have copied absolutely everything you need into the right eportfolio folders. Don't forget that a user will not be able to find evidence that is sitting in your user area!

Are my file formats acceptable?

Check the list of acceptable formats in THE PROJECT brief.

Am I happy with the pages?

The key to success now is to make full use of your storyboard.

Have I included the correct links?

Make sure that you have used the right links and that you can move between pages and look at all items.

Does it all work?

This is Step 9 on the flowchart. Refer to the checklist on page 154 and make sure that you can answer yes to every question.

Have I told the moderator enough?

Check that the information on each context page makes sense and includes enough detail.

What about the review?

You cannot complete the review just yet. You will work on this in Chapter 10.

10 Managing a project

It is easy to lose your way in a big project like the SPB. How will you make sure you finish on time?

The answer is simple: you need a plan!

This chapter will help you to produce and use a project plan.

A plan is like a road map: it helps you to get to where you want to go. In this case you want to get to the end of the SPB.

And when you get there, it is time to review the project.

Has it been a success? Did you do everything that was required? Are the final publications effective? What do other people think? What could you have done better?

All this will help you to gain useful skills in managing projects.

I've done it, Mr Bloggs

But the fete was 3 weeks ago!

In this chapter you will learn how to manage and review a project by:

► *producing a project plan*
► *using your plan to monitor your progress*
► *recording changes that you make to your plan*
► *reviewing how well the project went*

Failing to plan is planning to fail!

If you are going to stand any chance of completing a project on time, you need to plan. This is not as bad as it sounds. You do it all the time.

The SPB for Unit 1 is a big project, taking around 30 hours to complete. You cannot just plan it in your head. Follow the guidance below and you will not go far wrong.

> I need to hand in my Geography coursework by midday tomorrow. I just need to get that map I produced printed off at school

> I will get up 15 minutes earlier in the morning and go to the IT room before registration. I can then hand my folder in at break time

A simple plan, but it should work

Work out what is required

You need to identify:

▶ exactly what is required for the whole project: who, why, where, what, how

▶ all the main tasks and sub-tasks, including project planning, file management and end-of-project review

▶ the order in which you will carry out the tasks.

WHO WHY WHERE WHAT

HOW

▶▶ Activity 10.1

1 **Which SPB are you going to do? Check with your teacher and find it on the Edexcel website.**
2 **Working in a small group, discuss the brief for the SPB and create a mind map to show what is required. Show your mind maps to other groups and get feedback.**

Getting feedback

Getting feedback on your work is important. You should build it into your plan throughout the SPB. You should plan to get two main kinds of feedback:

Peer feedback. This means asking your classmates what they think of your work. Their feedback is very useful. Sometimes they will also be the target audience.

Feedback from test users. These are people who are like the target audience. If your publication is aimed at parents, try to use parents as test users. If your publication is aimed at primary school children, then your test users should be in that age group.

You need to:

▶ decide who you will ask for feedback

▶ decide when to ask them to look at your work

▶ put this into your plan.

Estimate the time needed

Estimating the time you need to do something can be difficult. You need to:

▶ decide how much time you will need for each task and sub-task

▶ check that you have allowed enough time

▶ check that you will meet the deadline.

TALKING POINT 10.1

What sort of tasks might take a lot more time than expected? Why?

You should discuss your planned timings with your teacher. You can make changes to your plan at any time as long as you make a note of why you changed it.

Working towards a plan

Your mind map from Activity 10.1 will help you draw up an outline plan of tasks and sub-tasks. Then you must decide:

▶ which tasks depend on others being finished first

▶ which can be worked on at the same time

▶ in what order you will do the tasks.

Here is a section of an outline plan for a survey:

Task	Sub-tasks
Prepare questionnaire	
	Draft
	Feedback and changes
Prepare spreadsheet	
	Draft
	Testing and changes
	Testing with questionnaire
	Feedback and changes
Survey	
	Conduct survey
	Put data into spreadsheet
	Analyse results

> **Activity 10.2**
>
> **Produce an outline plan for the Edexcel SPB.**

Producing a project plan

You have created an outline, so now you are almost ready to produce a detailed project plan. There are just a few other things to think about.

Check that every task is included

If something takes time, even a very short time, it should appear in your plan.

Create checkpoints

Checkpoints are where you stop and review your progress. Use your checkpoints to discuss progress with your teacher. Agree any changes you need to make. If you are going to make changes, you should update your plan.

Allow time for things to go wrong

There are always some unexpected problems. Build in some extra time to allow for this.

What does the project plan need to include?

There are no rules about what your project plan should look like. But it should clearly show:

- ▶ a start date and finish date for the project
- ▶ the project broken down into manageable tasks and sub-tasks
- ▶ time for file management, user feedback and review. These are all essential and carry marks!
- ▶ a logical order for the tasks and sub-tasks. Identify:
  - which items need to be completed before others begin
  - which things can be worked on at the same time
  - which things depend on availability of resources, such as cameras
- ▶ enough time for each task and sub-task with start and finish dates for each
- ▶ checkpoints where you discuss progress with your teacher
- ▶ changes you needed to make as you went along. Keep a record that you can refer back to. Use a 'Project log' or 'Comments' column for these.

Adding detail to the plan

A project plan can be done as a table using wordprocessing or spreadsheet software. Here is an extract from a project plan created from the outline plan on page 159.

	Task		Sub-tasks	Time needed	Comments
7	Prepare questionnaire				
		7.1	Draft	30 mins	
		7.2	Feedback and changes	15 mins	
8	Prepare spreadsheet				
		8.1	Draft	1 hour	Need to finish questionnaire first
		8.2	Testing and changes	30 mins	
		8.3	Testing with questionnaire	30 mins	
		8.4	Feedback and changes	20 mins	
9	Survey				
		9.1	Conduct survey	2 hours	Must follow 7 and 8
		9.2	Put data into spreadsheet	1 hour	
		9.3	Analyse results	1 hour	

The 'Time needed' column shows the number of hours or minutes allowed for each task.

In this case the 'Comments' column says when a task must be finished before the next one can be carried out. You can also use the 'Comments' column to record changes you make to the plan as you go along.

TALKING POINT 10.2

Do you think the student has allowed enough time for task 7.1 and 7.2? What might go wrong?

▸▸Activity 10.3

Open the outline plan you did in Activity 10.2.

1 **Give each task a number. Add columns for time needed and comments.**
2 **Now try to estimate the time you will need for each task. Think carefully and be realistic!**

Plan your work and work your plan!

The plan is not cast in stone – it can and will change.

Use it to monitor your progress so that you can see potential problems before they occur and take action.

The table can be used to monitor progress. Use columns for the 'Start date', one for the *planned* start date and one to show the *actual* start date. Use two columns for the 'Finish date' as well, one to show the *planned* finish date and one for the *actual* finish date.

In the example below, feedback on the questionnaire was late because the reviewer was ill. This held up completion of the spreadsheet.

The red row indicates a checkpoint where the student discussed progress with the teacher. As the final spreadsheet was late, the student agreed a plan to carry out the survey more quickly.

	Task	Sub-tasks	Time needed	Start date Planned	Start date Actual	Finish date Planned	Finish date Actual	Comments
7	Prepare questionnaire							
		7.1 Draft	30 mins	8 Jan	8 Jan	9 Jan	9 Jan	
		7.2 Feedback and changes	15 mins	10 Jan	10 Jan	12 Jan	15 Jan	*Reviewer was ill so this was delayed.*
8	Prepare spreadsheet	8.1 Draft	1 hour	8 Jan	8 Jan	12 Jan	15 Jan	Need to finish questionnaire first
		8.2 Testing and changes	30 mins	12 Jan	15 Jan	15 Jan	16 Jan	
		8.3 Testing with questionnaire	30 mins	16 Jan	17 Jan	17 Jan	18 Jan	
		8.4 Feedback and changes	20 mins	17 Jan	19 Jan	19 Jan	22 Jan	
9	Survey							
		9.1 Conduct survey	2 hours	22 Jan	23 Jan	26 Jan	26 Jan	Must follow 7 and 8
	9.2	Collate data	1 hour	29 Jan	29 Jan	30 Jan	30 Jan	
	9.3	Analyse results	1 hour	31 Jan	31 Jan	2 Feb	2 Feb	

TALKING POINT 10.3

The student finished task 9 on time even though he was delayed by three days at task 7.2. Where did he make up the time?

▸▸Activity 10.4

Look at this section from a different student's project plan.

1 In groups, discuss how you could improve the plan.

2 Open the file and make any necessary changes.

3 Swap your improved plans with another group and get feedback.

	Date	Task	Class time	Homework
1	29 Nov	Plan	Study SPB	Write task list
2	2 Dec	Plan	Produce plan	Produce plan
3	6 Dec	Initial plan Research Start research	Agree plan with teacher Continue research	
4	9 Dec	Eportfolio Research	Create structure chart and set up folders for eportfolio, Use internet for research	Continue research
5	13 Dec	Survey	Draft questionnaire	Work on questionnaire
6	16 Dec	Survey	Refine questionnaire Identify questionnaire target group	Design spreadsheet Approach people in target group
		CHRISTMAS HOLIDAY		
7	10 Jan	Spreadsheet	Set up spreadsheet Test questionnaire and spreadsheet together	Remind target group that I will be sending them questionnaire
8	13 Jan	Research	Print questionnaire **Put questionnaire evidence into eportfolio Update plan and journal**	Hand out questionnaires to be filled in. Draft leaflet

Choosing your software

A table can be produced using standard word processing or spreadsheet software. There are also many specialist programs for project planning. You may use one of these if you wish, but it is not a requirement for Unit 1.

No matter how you create it, you should be able to use your plan to track your progress and record any changes. Your plan must be clear and easy to use — and easy for other people to understand.

TALKING POINT 10.4

Discuss which application you will use to produce your project plan for the SPB.

How did it go?

Project review

You must carry out a review of the whole project. In your review you will:

▶ make sure that you really have done everything

▶ think about what went wrong and learn from your mistakes.

As well as reviewing your own performance, you should incorporate feedback from others: test users, your classmates and your teacher.

Using email to gather feedback

Email can be very efficient way of gathering feedback.

The final project review

At this point you must consider the project as a whole, as well as the individual publications. Look back at the project brief to remind yourself of what was required. In your review you should consider the project, the publications and your performance.

Part 1: The project as a whole

This part of the project review should answer these questions:

▶ What did the project set out to achieve?

▶ To what extent have you met the objectives?

▶ How well did your plan work?

▶ How well did you manage your time?

▶ Did you meet the deadlines?

▶ Did you choose the right people as your test users?

▶ What, if anything, went wrong?

▶ What improvements you would make if you had time?

▶ What you would do differently if you did the project again?

▶ What you have learned from working on the project?

TALKING POINT 10.5

How would you use email to get feedback from others? What are the advantages and disadvantages of getting feedback via email rather than at a face to face meeting?

TALKING POINT 10.6

This student is talking about how he used his project plan. Do you think this is a good way to review your work? How would you improve it?

Part 2: The publications

This part of the project review should answer these questions:

▶ Does each of the final publications get the right messages across to the intended audiences?

▶ How could the final publications be improved?

▶ Is the eportfolio easy to use?

▶ Is the information well presented?

▶ Did you include too little evidence ... or too much?

Part 3: How did you perform?

The review will help you learn from your experiences. It does not have to be very long. Ask yourself:

▶ What do you think of your final publications?

▶ What do you think of your performance on the project?

▶ What could you have done better?

▶ Have you learned things that you are using elsewhere?

▶ Are you proud of what you have achieved?

How will you go about the final project review?

Your review could be any combination of:

▶ a report   ▶ a table   ▶ a presentation

▶ a verbal evaluation recorded in sound or video.

If you are given a template in the SPB, use it but don't be afraid to change it if you want to.

Completing your eportfolio

When you have finished your review you can complete your eportfolio.

Make sure that all your review files are in acceptable formats. Copy them to the correct folders in your eportfolio.

Check that the overall size is still acceptable and then create links from the web pages to the review files. Check that the links work and then re-test the whole eportfolio.

Well done!

Tackling THE PROJECT

P

You've almost finished **THE PROJECT**. Now it's time to review how you did. Be honest with yourself!

Re-read at the 'Project review' section of **THE PROJECT**.

Final publications

You've already collected feedback on your final publications as you completed them. Use the **review document** in the 'Project review' section of **THE PROJECT** brief to record all your feedback on your final publications.

Final feedback

Ask reviewers for feedback on:

▶ **THE PROJECT** as a whole

▶ your eportfolio

▶ your performance.

Use the **review document** in the 'Project review' section of the brief to help you.

Reviewing your own performance

Using the **review document**, add your own assessment of:

▶ your publications

▶ **THE PROJECT** as a whole

▶ your eportfolio

▶ your performance.

Completing your eportfolio

Add your review file to your eportfolio. Make sure the file format is acceptable and the overall size of your eportfolio is still OK.

Now test, test and test again!

Congratulations! You've completed your eportfolio for **THE PROJECT**. When you do the real SPB, try to remember the lessons you've learnt.

The SPB and beyond

Well done! If you have made it this far, you will have completed your work on **THE PROJECT** and created your first eportfolio.

What happens next?

It's time to tackle the SPB.

Over the next few pages we will answer some frequently asked questions and give you some more information about how to gain as many marks as possible.

At the end of the chapter we take a look at some of the options for further study.

In this chapter, you will prepare for the next stage by:

► *learning more about tackling the SPB for Unit 1*
► *exploring what else DiDA has to offer*

Tackling the SPB

SPB stands for Summative Project Brief. Summative means this is the final assessment. Here are some answers to questions students often ask about the SPB.

Where will I find the SPB?

Look for the DiDA Summative Project Briefs on the Edexcel website. You will find lots of them, with different codes, so which is yours?

For Unit 1, Level 1 you should look for D101.

How long will I get?

You will have at least 30 hours of lesson time to work on the SPB. This is not a fixed amount of time and you can spend longer if your teacher agrees.

How much help will I get?

You cannot work in groups (except to collect data for the survey if your teacher agrees).

You must not copy what anyone else is doing.

Level 1 students can ask for help with some parts of the SPB. The less help you need, the more marks you can get.

Can I work on it at home?

You cannot work on your final publications at home. But there are lots of other jobs you might work on outside lesson time, such as planning, designing and getting feedback. You should show this on your project plan. Make sure your teacher agrees.

Who assesses it?

Your teacher will assess (mark) your eportfolio using a mark scheme provided by Edexcel.

Why do I need an eportfolio if my teacher is marking my work?

The skills you need to create an eportfolio are part of the course – over 20% of the marks are for the eportfolio itself.

DiDA moderators don't like paper. Your work must be sent to the moderator at Edexcel electronically.

What is a moderator?

A moderator is a DiDA expert employed by Edexcel to make sure that all teachers mark to the same standard. This means that everyone gets the marks they deserve.

Will the publications be the same as in THE PROJECT?

Not necessarily. THE PROJECT is bigger than an SPB. THE PROJECT helps you practise all the different skills that are included in the course.

An SPB is more specific. Each SPB has a different scenario. You only produce publications that are relevant to that scenario. Look at the SPBs on the Edexcel website. Read the scenarios.

Will I need to produce a plan this time?

Definitely! You will need a detailed project plan and you must use it. How else can you hope to get so much work done by the deadline?

	Date	Task	Class time	Homework
1	29 Nov	Plan	Study SPB	Write task list
2	2 Dec	Plan	Produce plan	Produce plan
3	6 Dec	Initial plan Research	Agree plan with teacher Start research	Continue research
4	9 Dec	Eportfolio Research	Create structure chart and set up folders for eportfolio, Use internet for research	Continue research
5	13 Dec	Survey	Draft questionnaire	Work on questionnaire

An extract from a project plan

Can I use components from the SPB in my own publications?

Of course you can, if they are relevant to what you have to say. Don't forget to acknowledge the source.

How will I know if I'm doing well?

Your project plan must include times for you to talk to your teacher about how things are going.

Your plan will also include getting feedback from classmates and test users. You can pair up with someone in your group and give each other regular feedback. Choose someone who will take the job seriously and give you honest feedback.

What do I do if I'm running out of time?

If you plan properly, then hopefully you won't run out of time. Avoid spending too long on some tasks at the expense of others. You may have to be satisfied with a less than perfect job if it is taking too long. Whatever you do, don't leave things out.

What will the moderator need to see?

The moderator will not know you and will not have seen you working on the SPB. He or she can only give you marks based on what they can see in your eportfolio. This is why it is so important to include all the things that are required.

What if some of my links don't work properly?

Even if the teacher has given you marks for something, the moderator cannot allow those marks if he or she cannot find the evidence. You must check that all your links work so the moderator can see your publications.

What if some of my files are in formats that are not acceptable?

Files in unacceptable formats will not be marked. You will lose marks for the eportfolio as well.

How many marks are there?

This table summarises how the marks work. The maximum mark is 42.

Level 1		
Mark out of 42	AiDA	Equivalent GCSE grade
36 – 42	Distinction	C
30 – 35	Merit	D
24 – 29	Credit	E
18 – 23	Pass	F/G

So how do I get marks?

The marking grid in the specification is divided into six sections. To get a particular mark in a section you must achieve *everything* listed for that mark. The marks for each section are added up to give the total.

TALKING POINT 11.1

In groups, look at the marking grid and discuss what you have to do to get marks in each section.

Look at the mark alerts in the SPB for helpful hints on how to improve your marks – and how to avoid losing them.

What if I leave something out?

You will almost certainly lose marks! How many depends on what has been left out.

> **TALKING POINT 11.2**
>
> *Look again at the marking grids for Level 1.*
>
> *Are there any questions you need to ask your teacher about the mark scheme?*

What if I'm really good at posters and leaflets but struggle with spreadsheets?

You must not ditch one in favour of the other. The marking grid shows that your final mark will depend on the quality of *both* of these. Do your best on all the publications.

> **TALKING POINT 11.3**
>
> *Discuss why it is important to stick to the project plan and have a go at everything.*
>
> *Look at the mark grids again and discuss what happens if you leave things out.*

What happens if someone copies my work?

Tell your teacher – you don't want to risk being accused of cheating. Moderators are trained to spot possible cases.

Can I resit the same SPB?

Yes you can – but you may have to start a new one. It's much better to put the effort in and do well the first time round.

Will I get AiDA even though I am going to do another unit?

You're only eligible for a certificate if you are claiming AiDA rather than doing Unit 1 as part of a CiDA or DiDA.

Where next?

All units build on Unit 1 so you are now in a good position to tackle more units.

You can do different units at a mixture of levels. For example, if you have done Unit 1 at Level 1, you could do Unit 2 at Level 1 or 2.

If you are going to work towards CiDA or DiDA, you will need to make a start on one of the other units. Each unit is assessed by an SPB and you must submit your work in an eportfolio.

We are going to take a look at the first three units available. To find out more, visit the Edexcel website. While you are there, check out what other units are available. By the time you read this there may well be more options.

Unit 2: Multimedia

You are surrounded by multimedia — when you browse a website, play a video game, download an MP3 file, use a mobile phone or watch a DVD. Multimedia is any combination of text, images, sound, video and interactive components, such as buttons.

TALKING POINT 11.4

Can you explain what is meant by multimedia? Why is multimedia used?

What multimedia publications did you produce for **THE PROJECT** *for Unit 1?*

▸▸ Activity 11.1

Look at the list of skills you will need before you tackle the SPB for Unit 2. What do you know already?

If you study Unit 2, you will learn how to plan, design, build and test more complex multimedia products — not only web pages and presentations, but other products such as virtual tours, interactive quizzes, movie trailers, presentations and e-books.

TALKING POINT 11.5

What multimedia products have you used recently? Were they all fit for purpose? Or were some of them not very good?

The production cycle is the same for all units. Testing using prototypes will be vital.

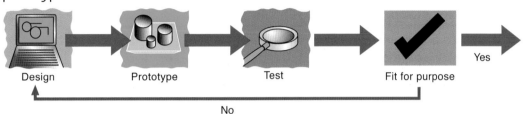

Design → Prototype → Test → Fit for purpose → Yes

No

Most exciting of all, you will be able to make the eportfolio an interactive multimedia showcase for your work.

Unit 3: Graphics

Can you imagine a world without images? Think how they are used to promote products and services. And where would computer games and the internet be without them?

Again you will be able to build on your experiences in Unit 1. You have learned the basics of putting images into publications for screen and print.

▶▶Activity 11.2

Look at the list of skills you will need before you tackle the SPB for Unit 3. What do you know already?

If you study Unit 3, you will learn to use graphics software creatively and effectively. You will learn to plan, design and create graphics components for use in various products and publications.

▸▸ Activity 11.3

Collect some examples of computer art and graphics from magazines. Can you find examples of pages with little or no text? How do the images help to get the message across?

TALKING POINT 11.6

Choose an organisation or product that interests you – a pop group, football team, well-known brand of food or clothing, etc. How are images used to promote them? Where do you see these images?

Whether you want to produce stunning computer art or simply want to get your message across without words, this unit is for you.

Your eportfolio will be an exciting gallery for your work.

TALKING POINT 11.7

How might Unit 3 help you with other subjects? Don't just think about art and design subjects. What about biology? Or sport?

What jobs might allow you to use graphics skills?

Unit 4: ICT in Enterprise

Have you ever thought about starting your own business? Or organising a big event? Enterprise is about turning an idea into a successful venture.

▸▸ Activity 11.4

Look at the list of skills you will need to be able to tackle the SPB for Unit 4. What do you know already?

TALKING POINT 11.8

Think about some successful enterprises, some that are intended to make a profit and some that are not. What makes them work? Think about different aspects – finance, marketing, customer service, etc.

If you study Unit 4, you will learn how to plan enterprise opportunities using ICT. You will also learn how to produce marketing materials and other publications. You will develop your spreadsheet skills so that you can check out what will happen in different situations – more customers, higher prices, etc. – to make sure the enterprise does not make a loss.

TALKING POINT 11.9

Look at an SPB for Unit 4 on the Edexcel website. What do you think about it? Which aspects appeal to you the most? Which aspects do you think would be most challenging?

For the SPB you will research and plan for the launch of a business enterprise. Your eportfolio will be an e-business plan. It will contain everything needed to convince someone that your enterprise can be a success.

TALKING POINT 11.10

How useful might this unit be? How might you use the skills and knowledge in:

▶ *other subjects that you study*

▶ *things you do outside of school or college?*

Skills list

Artwork and imaging tools

Scan an image	41
Change the settings for a scan	41
Crop and resize scanned text and images	41
Use a digital camera	41
Optimise images*	104

Database tools

Enter information	74
Edit information	74
Delete information	74
Change layout on a data entry form	74
Create a data entry form	75
Select fields for the form	75
Change colours and formatting	75
Enter a suitable title	75
Enter labels	75
Edit validation messages*	77
Search on a single field	80
Search on more than one field*	80
Use relational operators	80
Use logical operators	80
Select fields to include in results	80
Sort on one field	80
Create a report	126
Customise a report	126

Note: Skills marked * are optional at Level 1.

Email

File management tools

Internet and intranets

Presentation tools

Spreadsheet tools

Website authoring tools

Word processing tools

Index

Edexcel
190 High Holborn
London WC1V 7BH

© Edexcel 2006

The right of Elaine Topping, Ann Weidmann and Marilyn Hartwell to be identified as the authors of this work has been asserted by them in accordance with the Copyright, Designs and Patents Act of 1988.

ISBN-10: 1-84690-121-9
ISBN-13: 978-1-84690-121-8

Designed by Peter and Jan Simmonett
Picture research by Ann Thomson
Illustrated by David Shenton and Tony Wilkins
Index by Indexing Specialists (UK) Ltd

Printed and bound in Great Britain by CPI Bath

The publisher's policy is to use paper manufactured from sustainable forests,

Acknowledgements

We are grateful to the following for permission to reproduce photographs and illustrations:
A1pix: pg 27, pg 92, pg 123, pg 135 (J. Alexandre); **Abode:** pg 122 (T. Imrie); **Alamy:** pg 17(t) (Black Star), pg 21(t) (D. Hoffman Photo Library), pg 74, pg 124 (Royalty Free), pg 85 (t), pg 90(t) (Shoosh/Up The Res), pg 91 (Cuneyt Kizilelma)(draganddrop), pg 129 (bl) (Photofusion), pg 137(b) (Ace Stock Ltd), pg 152 (Dynamic Graphics Group/Creatas); **BAA Aviation Picture Library:** pg 1(t); **Camera Press:** pg 172(l) (H. Miyata), pg 172(r) (C. Bresciani); **Corbis:** pg 4, pg 36, pg 47(b),pg 69 (t) (royalty-free), pg 5(r) (LWA-D. Tardif), pg17(b) (H. Rune/Sygma), pg 18(b), pg 24(r) (R. Klune), pg 45(r) (Owaki-Kulla), pg 127(t) (J. Luis Pelaez Inc.) ; **Dorling kindersley:** pg 24(l) (M. Alexander), pg 91; **Education Photos:** pg 175(r) (J. Walmsley); **Empics:** pg 48 (F. Matthew-Fearn); **Epson UK Ltd:** pg 173(r); **Getty Images:** pg 23(t) (R. Estakhrian), pg 31(br) (C. Zachariasen), pg 47(t) (Sparky), pg 65(t) (J.W. Banagan), pg 65(br) (M. Schlossman), pg 85(br) (T. Page), pg 95(t) (S. Johnson), pg 111(t) (VCL/S. Rowell), pg 137(t) (T. Anderson), pg 157(t) (Photodisc), pg 159 (M. York), pg 167(t) (S. McAlister); **Guzelian:** pg 173(l) (J. Russell); **Hemera Photo-Objects:** pg 25 (br), pg 35 (t); **Hideaways:** pg 70; pg 91 (draganddrop); **Image Source Ltd:** pg 167(b); **Masterfile:** pg 23(b) (H. Vu); **Pearson Education:** pg 18(t) (*Digitexts: The Lost Boy*); **Photographersdirect.com:** pg 12 (S. Kujawa Images), pg 22 (P. Glendell Photography); **Punchstock:** pg 25 (bl), pg 40, pg 99 (Digital Vision), pg 98 (Photodisc), pg117 (Photodisc); pg 129 (pixland); **Robertharding:** pg 175(l) (BananaStock); **Solihull Metropolitan Borough Council:** pg 20 (b); **Superstock:** pg 31(t) (Digital Vision Ltd), pg 111(b) (age fotostock); **Topfoto:** pg 53 (J. Greenberg/ The Image Works).

The following photographs were taken on commission © **Pearson Education Ltd:** pg 1(br), pg 20 (t), pg 50, pg 52, pg 85(br), pg 95(br), pg 104(b), **(by Trevor Clifford):** pg 38(b), pg 39, pg 66, pg 67(t).

We wish to thank the following sources for the use of their website information and other copyright material:

adultlearning.co.uk; The BBC; beetrootblue.com; Boots Group plc; Broadway Cinema Ltd; *Cine*world Cinemas; Lewes District Council; The Countryside Agency; Cresta Hospitality Hotel Group; Andy Darvill; Dicoll Limited; Food Standards Agency; gastroblog.com; Glasgow Museums; Google Inc.; Hideaways; Inform; HMSO for permission to reproduce *Every Child Matters: What do you think?*, published on the Every Child Matters website at www.everychildmatters.gov.uk; Interflora; King's College Hospital; London Fire Brigade; Microsoft Corporation; The National Trust; Northumberland National Park Authority; NSPCC; scream.co.uk Ltd; Scrimsign Micro-Electronics Ltd; Shropshire County Council; Office for National Statistics; PhotoDisc®; Solihull Metropolitan Borough Council; Stourport Town Centre Forum; Tesco Stores Ltd; UNICEF; Waverley Railway Project; Wiltshire Farm Foods; Yellow Pages; The National Youth Agency

Microsoft, Word, Excel, PowerPoint, Access, FrontPage and Internet Explorer are trademarks of the Microsoft Corporation. Dreamweaver is a trademark of Macromedia, Inc. Google is a trademark of Google Inc. Mozilla Firefox is a trademark of the Mozilla Foundation.

Every effort has been made to trace and acknowledge ownership of copyright and we apologise in advance for any unintentional omissions. If any have been overlooked we would be pleased to insert the appropriate acknowledgement at the earliest opportunity.